Check the Gauges

Brent Bailey

ISBN-10:
0692850589

ISBN-13:
978-0692850589 (Brent Bailey)

Thanks & Dedication

Well, here it is. My first book. I can't say that this was easy, but I can say that the contents are what God has laid on my heart. I've seen so many people begin their walk with the Lord and become disillusioned. I don't believe that I have written the end-all to this challenge, but I believe this book will help some of them. I want to thank and dedicate this book to some folks who, outside of my walk with the Lord, made this possible. First and foremost, my wife, Jodi: thank you for doing this with me. Pastoring together, our life together, our achievements together, and our family together is an amazing thing that I do not feel worthy of. You are a treasure and I love you. To my sons, Preston and Peyton, you two changed me in ways you won't understand until you have children of your own. I'm so grateful to God for you being the greatest gifts your mother and I have ever received. This book is dedicated to you three.

I also want to thank my parents, J.P. and Nancy, who gave me life, raised me in a great home, in a great hometown, and in a great church. You have given me an incredible heritage that I wouldn't trade for anything. To the Bailey/Caudill family, what a legacy of faith! I don't even know how to express it. Over 30 ministers came out of our family. WOW! You all are incredible and were shining examples of godliness, faith, support, and fun while growing up. To my mom's side of the family, the Nigra/Mullins, I never laughed as much growing up as I did around all of you. Thank you for being real and keeping me in touch with the real world. Thank you to Jodi's family, the Cooks/Matthews. It is awesome when you don't have the awkwardness of strained relationships with in-laws. You all have always been so supportive and given me something I never had growing up; siblings, which also made me an uncle! Even though you all are special to me, I must admit Brian and I have made fools of ourselves too much in front of too many people to not mention him by name. YOU ARE MY BROTHER! I love all of you so much.

In ministry, there have been people who painted large strokes of influence in my life and showed me more of who God is. Thank you first to Pastor Ken and Lynette Hagin. What an honor it was to serve Kenneth Hagin Ministries/Rhema Bible Church on the pastoral staff and instructor at Rhema Bible Training College for 11 years. Your example of faith and integrity were so impactful. A big thank you to Bob Harrison for giving me a chance to learn and grow while serving your ministry at the Increase events. My thinking has been expanded greatly for increase. I also want to thank my pastors growing up, Brother Wells Bloomfield, Brother James Wells, Brother Tom Geissinger, and Pastor Don Adkins for pastoring a small church in Flatwoods, Kentucky. This church was *the* best place to grow up and know God. Thank you for using an incredible lady named Ruth Bradley in the church's nursery that introduced the story of Jesus to me for the first time. I am a product of the ministry of Ruth, first and foremost, and of course, all of you incredible men who pastored our church. I also am thankful for Rita Robinson, Todd Bailey, and my Uncle Dwight Bailey who all served as my youth pastors at some time in my life. You believed in me and saw a calling in me when I was very young and all of you encouraged me to go and be what God called me to be!

It's impossible to be in ministry if you don't have friends, or else it's a lonely road. I have a few that made incredibly large impacts! Keith Nachbor (pronounced neighbor), God knew what He was doing when He brought us together. We worked our hind ends off, shook the gates of hell, molded some next generation youth pastors, and helped shape a generation of teenagers to know God themselves. Thanks for speaking wisdom and sound advice into my life and helping me become the next phase of who I was supposed to become. There has been nobody I have enjoyed being creative with more than you! Looking forward to the next time!

For Jerm, the best man at my wedding and I had the honor to officiate yours. I am so proud of you and who you became with your life, Sergeant. We grew up together and a lot of what I preach about is from experiences with you. One day maybe we can spend another full day playing video games on the couches in the living room (cue the wheezing and cackle laughter!).

To Jeff Bardel, Aaron Bailey, Craig Hagin, Dan Taylor, Josh Huffman, Hammy Gresham, Jeremy Adkins, Dave Vasquez, and Anthony Storino: you guys are incredible friends who I know I could call on tomorrow and you would drop everything (well maybe not Aaron), and come running! I love you guys and appreciate you so much for the conversations, good times, chances to minister together, and just being my friends.

To my former youth groups, ALL STARS in Kentucky, and AXIS at Rhema, it was an honor being your youth pastor as you were growing up. I am proud of who many of you turned out to be. Thank you for allowing me to speak into your life. You guys *are* world changers and I am proud to have known you when you were just starting out in your purpose. To Synergy, thank you for being the place where I transitioned from youth ministry into adult ministry. I still think back to the Peanut Butter Burger at LEON's and that incredible single's conference! To the congregation of Faith Christian Assembly and Rhema Bible Church, what can I say? You have always been incredible and supporting! Thank you for allowing me to serve and come home whenever I want, and always feel welcome!

Lastly, I want to thank the congregation and my current family at Direction Church. This **#journeytogether** with you is something I still cannot believe is happening. When we opened the doors in 2012, I was nervous and went home afterwards with my parents and Jodi saying, "I cannot believe that just happened." You are such a loving, supportive, and diverse group of believers that Jodi and I love having a relationship with. I am very proud of you and what you are doing and becoming. Thank you for allowing me to be your pastor!

Acknowledgments
Editor: Jeff Bardel
Cover Art: Amber Warner
Internal Fuel Gauge Art: Mike Roell
Proof reader: Dr. Janet Kline DD

Works referenced:

The Amplified Bible: Containing the Amplified Old Testament and the Amplified New Testament. Grand Rapids, MI: Zondervan, 1995. Print.

"Bible Gateway." *New King James Version (NKJV) - Version Information - BibleGateway.com*. Thomas Nelson, n.d. Web. 18 Feb. 2017.

"Dictionary.com." *Dictionary.com*. Dictionary.com, n.d. Web. 18 Feb. 2017.

Dobson, Roger, and Fiona MacRae. "Why Meals Make Tricky Topics Easier to Digest: Study Finds People Get on Better with Each Other When They Eat Together." *Daily Mail Online*. Associated Newspapers, 14 Apr. 2015. Web. 30 Apr. 2015.

Easton, Matthew G. "Covenant." *Easton Bible Dictionary*. Third ed. 1897. Print.

"Encyclopedia Judaica Online." *Bureau of Jewish Education Inc*. N.p., n.d. Web. 18 Feb. 2017.

Hamilton, Jon. "The Forgotten Childhood: Why Early Memories Fade." *NPR*. NPR, 8 Apr. 2014. Web. 30 Apr. 2015.

"Huge List of English Bible Translations." *Huge List of English Bible Translations*. Robert Young, n.d. Web. 18 Feb. 2017.

Roland, McCraty, PhD, Mike Atkinson, Dana Tomasino, BA, and Wiliam A. Tiller, PhD. "The Electricity of Touch: Detection and Measurement of Cardiac Energy Exchange between People." (1998): n. pag. Web.

Strongs, James. "Strong's Hebrew: 3942." *Biblehub.com*. Bible Hub, n.d. Web. 30 Apr. 2015. <http://biblehub.com/hebrew/3942.htm>.

Weinfeld, Moshe. "Covenant." *Go.galegroup.com*. MacMillan Reference, 2007. Web. 30 Apr. 2015.

"Zondervan." *Zondervan*. N.p., n.d. Web. 18 Feb. 2017.

CONTENTS

Preface

The Bible introduces us to a very interesting event that is going to happen in the Church as we get closer to the last days. That concept is this: The Church will have people in its walls that will look like normal Christians, but will not be fully reliant on the power of God that it takes to live the full Christian life. They will deny that this power even exists or they will not apply this power to their lives. Paul told Timothy, who was a young, hip pastor of one of the largest churches in existence at that time, that this was coming.

2 Timothy 3:1–5 (NLT) You should know this, Timothy, that in the last days there will be very difficult times. For people will love only themselves and their money. They will be boastful and proud, scoffing at God, disobedient to their parents, and ungrateful. They will consider nothing sacred. They will be unloving and unforgiving; they will slander others and have no self-control. They will be cruel and hate what is good. They will betray their friends, be reckless, be puffed up with pride, and love pleasure rather than God. *They will act religious, but they will reject the power that could make them godly.* Stay away from people like that!

Timothy was the pastor of the church at Ephesus. This church was the place that the Apostle John and Jesus' mother, Mary, attended regularly at one time. What a snapshot of some of our large churches today; successful churches with young, hip pastors who are attracting celebrities and dignitaries. Let me clarify, I am not against that at all. I believe the Church should have that large of a reach. Our influence should attract everyone from the lowest of the low to the most successful, because the message we preach is the greatest message of hope and healing that there is. People who are hurting can experience relief. People who are lost and confused can find answers. People who are depressed can experience joy. People who are addicted can be delivered. People in need can have supply. Our churches should be delivering this message as loud and as frequently as we can because it is life changing and it shouldn't surprise us when that influence touches the biggest of the big.

I guess what I'm beginning this book by saying is *the church today isn't that much different than it was back then.* There were large hip churches pastored by young rising stars like Timothy as well as large, conservative churches pastored by pillars of the church like Peter and James. Regardless if they are a young "seeker-friendly" church with a hip young pastor and celebrity-rich congregation, or a conservative hardline church with a traditional pastor who still wears a suit and tie, there is a time coming, and I believe it may already be here, that the church will have people in it that are denying the power of God that will change them.

It is easy to believe that people will be arrogant and combative and will rise-up denying God's power to change them. I do not believe every one of these people will be denying the power that "could make them godly" on purpose, or out of contempt for the things of God. I believe some of them, maybe even most of them, will deny God's power by crumbling under the pressure of challenges they will face. I believe some of them will have three things working against them.

Number one, their ignorance of what God's Word says. They simply do not know what God says about them. Number two, they do not spend a lot of quality time with God in prayer because they don't know how to pray, they lack the confidence to pray, or they don't see the point in praying. Number three, they look at life through rose-colored glasses. They believe that now that they are saved everything will just happen or that it is not supposed to be this hard. These three things set them up for failure.

Aren't we seeing that in our churches now? Sincere people come to church, raise their hands, worship God, cry, go to small group, drink coffee in the lobby with an open Bible and a friend, have their favorite worship album (traditional, southern gospel, or modern—it doesn't matter) on repeat in their car, and even complete discipleship and membership classes. The next thing you know they disappear or become inconsistent in their walk with God and go back to their old way of doing things. What happened? I believe they *tried* Jesus and *tried* being a Christian. But to experience change, God's power must be fully implemented as a way of life and not just *tried.*

Even though the Bible shows us that these people will and do exist, I want to make it clear that you don't have to be one of them. I believe that while there *will* be people denying God's power, at the same time the church *will* have a bright and shining moment. There will be a time where people, filled with God's power and love, will make a real difference in the world. How will this kind of moment happen? Those people that are filled will be fervently relying on ***"the power that could make them godly."***

In life, everyone has a time where they are seeking answers. Sometimes people grab the answer and start running only to get bored or discouraged, and quit. They stop trying and walk away from their quest for the answers. They jump from career to career, relationship to relationship, location to location, and sometimes church to church, only to bail out and move on to the next one every time things get hard or are not as exciting as it once was. These people, with these challenges, continue to experience those same challenges throughout their whole life, never finding the answer they are seeking.

In contrast, there are people who grab the answer firmly. When the same challenges, boredom, or discouragements arise, they keep pushing until they reach a full understanding of what is happening in their lives. They may realize they've made a mistake and possibly end up switching tracks anyway, but these people are not quitters. These types of people have been instrumental in changing the world. I am thankful they refused to stop seeking answers to life's challenges. Their perseverance in seeking God has taught others to *never stop* their quest for answers.

In this book, I want to encourage you in your walk with God to press through the awkward, hard, and dry times. *A relationship with God will only be as good as you make it!* It's not going to just happen. Certainly, there are hard and challenging times where we don't understand what we are facing. These are times when we pray and it feels as if our prayers are not being answered. We open our Bible and the words tend to run together and not make sense. We go to church and someone offends us with their judgmental, old-fashioned irrelevance or watered down, seeker-sensitive arrogance. We try to be good, but temptation overwhelms us. We get fired from our job. Our best friend moves away. A family member dies. We are diagnosed with an illness. We are involved in a wreck. The list just keeps on going.

We need to stop and understand that these challenges are a part of the journey and they are always going to be there. It is *still* God's desire for us to live and experience a full Christian life. Within our very beings, God has placed a spiritual gauge that can lead us through every one of life's challenges. If we learn to check those gauges regularly, we can do what the apostle Paul told Titus:

TITUS 3:8 (NKJV) This is a faithful saying, and these things I want you to affirm constantly, that those who have believed in God should be careful to *maintain good works*. These things are good and profitable to men.

Regardless of where you are on your spiritual journey—whether you are just beginning, in the middle, or near the completion of that journey—the insights from this book may be eye-opening. Maybe you're coming to a crossroads where you realize you should make changes. In that case, the information within this book may be helpful but elementary. Wherever you are, it is my sincere hope that the information contained within these pages may serve as a reminder to keep you focused on overcoming challenges that you may face in achieving the life God intends for you. Whatever the case may be in your life, my prayer is that this book will be a great help so that you will draw closer to Jesus than you ever have before. The Church will not become the bright and shining light, based on the success or fame of our pastors and ministers. The Church will *only* shine its brightest when *you* live for God and are constantly filled with the power that "makes you godly!" With that said, let's fill 'er up!

Introduction

"It's 3:00 a.m. God!"

I want to start by telling you a story about an experience I had in the middle of the night. In 2012, Jodi and I left Oklahoma where I was working at my dream job. I had the privilege of working there for 11 years. I was doing ministry on a level I never dreamed I would reach. I was a youth pastor and young adult pastor in a megachurch as well as an instructor at a Bible college. Working for this internationally-known ministry was a dream come true. The level of ministry brought resources, access to people, and opportunities to preach in places I had never visited before. Being a part of that ministry revolutionized my thinking and my life. It was the place that I always wanted to work. The decade I worked for that ministry flew by more quickly than you could snap your fingers.

When my time at that ministry ended, my wife and I ventured out to plant a new church. We packed up all our possessions and moved from Tulsa, Oklahoma, to Orlando, Florida, to begin the journey of pioneering Direction Church. This experience was scary and exciting all at the same time. I was learning to live by faith more than I ever had before. To step out and begin a new adventure in life with no guarantees was sobering to say the least. There was no safety net, no back-up plan, no secular job in place, no existing congregation we were taking over, and no mother church fully backing us, directing us, or planting us. It was just a feeling on the inside that we believed was God leading us to start a church.

Just like anything in life that is beginning, starting a church is hard. The challenges that come are expected, but then pioneering brings its own set of challenges many other projects do not bring. The feelings of loneliness, rejection, and worry were constantly being confronted. The pressure of financial strain—on the church and us as a family—was a consistent burden that was trying to attach itself to us. The other thing was the fact that many folks just did not understand that a newly planted church does not have the same structure and resources of an established church. Because of this, potential members would bail quickly, thinking we should do things a certain way.

It was a treadmill of new faces. These people often believed we should do things the same way other churches were doing it. They often didn't have the common sense to know we couldn't do things the way other churches did because we were so limited on people and resources. Many times, the thought crossed my mind to just forget the entire thing and quit because it didn't feel like it was worth it. But within this struggle to establish something that never existed, I had an experience I will never forget.

I believe with everything in me that it was a supernatural and spectacular experience that God used to show me a few things in a vivid and crystal-clear way. I am not someone who has claimed to hear the actual voice of the Lord, although I do believe He speaks to people. I don't put a lot of stock in just anyone's dreams and visions, even though I do believe God speaks and shows things to people in that way.

In my family, we are slanted towards ministry. I've had over 30 cousins, uncles, aunts, and great-grandparents who have been in ministry. I've had family members who have had dreams and visions of heaven and conversations with angels and those who have died and gone to heaven. In my experience of working at the large international ministry, we constantly heard stories of the founder of that ministry who had several visions and conversations with Jesus. Those visions produced a lot of obvious fruit. I firmly believe these things are real, but I don't believe they are the norm.

I have always believed in the inward witness and that the leading of the Spirit is the vehicle through which God speaks to His people the most. I look back on almost every leading of the Holy Spirit in my life and realize the leading was simply "knowing" that whatever we were going to do was the right thing. I have not had a lot of so called "spectacular" leadings throughout my life. By spectacular, I mean more than the inward witness or a scripture that seems to jump off the page. I do believe the non-spectacular leadings are still very supernatural, since they are coming from the Lord. However, the spectacular vision, or dream, or visitation has rarely happened to me. I have, however, had a few.

One night something happened that changed the way I pastor, minister, deal with people, and live my life. That event encouraged me not to give up. It was the answer that I needed. It was a clear message of direction for our church and for people who are going to live their life for God.

We were going through a season in our church where the Lord began to deal with us to prepare for something hard that was going to happen. During that time, He led me to study the story of Joseph when he was the prime minister over Egypt. When Joseph was a young man, God gave him a dream that he would be exalted to such a place of honor and strength that even his family would end up bowing down to him. He made the mistake of sharing the dream with his family. What family would ever want to hear that? Joseph had a horrible few years of being rejected by his brothers. This relationship with them went on such a downward spiral, that they sold him into slavery. They lied to their father and told him Joseph had been killed. As if that wasn't bad enough, he then got falsely accused of sexual harassment and was thrown in prison only to be forgotten about.

Joseph stuck with his commitment to God and finally got his chance to rise to the place God had designed for him years earlier in his dream. He was brought before Pharaoh to explain some weird dreams that the King had. The short version was that Joseph told Pharaoh that seven good years were coming. These seven good years would have plenty of crops and food for everyone, with enough left over to be stored. After these seven good years, there would be seven horrible years of famine where there would be no food, no crops, and there would not be enough for everyone.

Joseph told Pharaoh to prepare and ration the excess from the years of plenty so the land could be sustained. If done properly, Egypt would come through the seven years of famine just fine. Joseph was then promoted to prime minister of Egypt and assigned to be the leader who would bring them through this 14-year span. If you want to read the whole story, it's found in the Old Testament in Genesis chapters 37–47. It's a great story of restoration, family, dreams, and preparation.

As I studied this story, I knew we were going to go through a rocky time. In this rocky time, we'd be fine if we prepared ourselves in the way the Holy Spirit instructed. The only problem was I didn't know how to prepare specifically because I didn't know exactly what the challenge was going to be. In sports, battle, work, school tests, or life, if you know what you are preparing to do, it is much easier to prepare. Teams watch films, governments have spies, schools have review and tutors, and jobs have training. Preparation is a part of life. It has often been said, "Preparation time is never wasted time."

This time, however, all I knew was that we needed to prepare for a rough time that was coming. I had no idea of the source of the challenge. We began doing what we knew to do, in the best way we knew to do it, and sure enough, in the seventh month of the year, we got hit. But thank God, we had already started making changes. One day, the one I believe was the worst, God gave me some specific things to change. Those changes would be part of our preparation. That day we had four families tell us they were leaving the church.

We were still a new church and having four families leave us was a huge blow to our infant and fragile church. My world felt like it was collapsing. (Flash forward—only two ended up leaving and we rebounded successfully.) I finally calmed down and unwound enough to go to bed. I fell asleep praying and asking God what I needed to do, to change, and to fix. I had all kinds of other people telling me a variety of different things, but I said to God, "You're going to have to show me what I need to do. Nobody else can tell me in a way that clicks for me, except for You. I refuse to be led by people's desires and thoughts for the church and ministry. I want to be led by the Holy Spirit. I have tradition and upbringing pulling me in one direction. Coaching and books are pulling me in another direction. And the desire of opinionated people pulling me in another. I have to hear from You what will work for me."

(That's a good lesson to learn. If you have a relationship with God, anything anyone else tells you should be a confirmation of what the

Holy Spirit is leading you to do already. If what they say surprises you, and God hasn't already been dealing with you about it, it's probably not Him leading you. Also, just because you read it in a book, heard your favorite speaker say it, or you heard "this way" is the rave, does not mean that's how you "*have to*" do it. Find out what will work for you. You aren't supposed to be a carbon copy of someone else's life. Listen to the leading of the Holy Spirit and what He is leading *you* to do. Lastly, lose the excuse that you were raised that way. What if the way you were raised was wrong? God knows what He needs You to be and what He expects from you, and if you'll listen to Him, He will lead you in the way that is the most successful for you and your life.)

Now, back to my story. I fell asleep praying when suddenly I felt someone sit down on the couch where I had fallen asleep. We had just moved into a new home and both of my sons, seven and three at the time, were sleeping in our room because they hadn't gotten used to this strange new house. In our new bedroom, we had room enough for a couch and chair in a sitting area, so I had settled on the couch to give everyone a little room in the bed until the adjustment to our new surroundings was over. I remember it very vividly. It was 3:00 a.m. and it felt like one of my boys had climbed onto the couch where my feet were. I jumped up thinking I would help them get settled, but to my surprise nobody was there. Both boys and Jodi were sound asleep in the bed. I heard the leading, not the voice, of the Lord say, "Sit back down." When I sat back down, I was instantly somewhere else. I was having a vision or a dream. (*I told you this was spectacular. Someone may feel better calling it a dream and I'm okay with that. Whatever it was that I experienced, God spoke to me through it, and it changed me.*)

In this vision/dream, I knew I was in a church somewhere. I don't know where, but I saw large crowds of people coming through the doors of the church. What made this so unusual was the fact that I could see right through these people. I could see their faces, what they looked like, and what kind of clothes they were wearing, but still see through them like a ghost. It reminded me of the phantoms on Scooby-Doo and Saturday morning cartoons I watched as a kid. I could almost hear that old theme song in my head. But in the process of seeing through these people, their insides appeared to me like a fuel gauge from a 1980s car. The fuel gauge looked digital with four distinct quarter-of-a-tank marks. The thing that was so alarming was nobody was coming into the church full—not one person.

Nearly all of them were coming in on empty with a flashing "E." A few were coming in one quarter filled and fewer still were coming in half filled. Nobody came in more than half full. I immediately understood this to mean that these people were either full or empty, spiritually speaking. The most alarming part of this was that most people are coming through the doors of the church empty.

I wholeheartedly believe we should see most of the people that come to our churches for the first time as empty. But the people I was seeing weren't just first-timers. There were a lot of first timers, but there were some people who had a relationship with Jesus for years. These people were also coming in empty. How did I know they had been saved for years? I recognized some of them. It was at this point I heard a voice. I don't know for certain if it was God's voice or not, but the voice said, "So many people are depending on the Church to fill them all the way up and they're showing up to church empty. Their dependence on the

Church to fill them is setting them up for a disappointment because that is not the job of the Church. Not only is this thinking wrong by people showing up empty, but it is just as wrong for pastors to believe their job is to keep people filled through their church services."

When I was 16 and starting to drive, I had a 1987 Pontiac Firebird that closely resembled KITT from the television show *Knight Rider*. I loved that car, but my goodness, it required a lot of gasoline. By today's standards, it would be painful to drive. However, in those days gas was $.89 a gallon, and I worked for my uncle's grocery store making $3.35 per hour. I was ever so grateful when my parents told me they were willing to give me their gas card one day a week to fill up. If I used all of that, I had to put gas in the tank myself.

I remember the first Friday I got their card. I went all over the place cruising with my friends, but on Monday there was less than one quarter of a tank left. There was no way those eight cylinders were going to allow the tank to keep gas in it until Friday unless I didn't drive it anywhere. So, guess what I did? I only drove to school, football practice, and home. I had no gas for extra-curricular activities because I didn't want to use my own money to fill up my car. I wanted to be dependent on "free gas" so I could spend my money on whatever I wanted to: pizza, burgers, movies, video games, and everything else teenagers of the 80's were into.

This all came rushing back to my remembrance as this dream showed me people's mindsets. There were primarily two mindsets from the people in the dream. There was a third, but much smaller mindset and an even smaller fourth mindset as well.

The first mindset belongs to people who are solely depending on the Church to keep them spiritually filled up—they are sitting around doing nothing spiritually, on their own. They read their Bible very little, pray even less, do not serve in the local church at all, and tithing is a completely foreign concept. They attend service whenever they want. They look at their walk with God through the lens of what their church is doing. The success of their church is their barometer of their spiritual growth. If the church is doing something awesome, they are doing awesome. If the church is popular, they are happy. Their church's success dictates their spiritual reality when in fact it has nothing to do with it. These people are not growing spiritually and are still just as clueless as when they first got saved.

The second mindset belongs to people who are being selfish with what they receive in church because they need every bit of what the "preacher" says to get them through the rest of the week. These people are not confident in their walk with God and they think they don't know enough about the things of God to make a difference in the world. They are saving what they learn from church for themselves only. They also don't care or don't believe they could help someone else anyway, so they don't share what they receive with anyone else.

The third mindset is people who are lazy and not interested in filling themselves. They give every excuse to explain why they can't fill themselves with the things of God. They do not even care enough to fill themselves back up. They are barely making it back to church on Sunday with their salvation intact.

The fourth mindset is people who take the initiative to feed themselves, fill themselves with the Word, develop a prayer life, and do all the things the first group will not do. These people are growing in their relationship with God, growing in their understanding of His Word, and producing fruits of the Spirit in all areas of their lives.

People with the first three mindsets have misunderstood how their relationship with God works. People have replaced this relationship with a living God with a religious idea of who God is. They also never get to know God because they are too busy following rules and going to church. Many allow themselves to think the Church is the answer.

I am not here to bash on the Church or communicate some crazy thing that the Church is irrelevant. I believe in the Church. The Church knows many of the answers and desperately wants to share them with others, but at the same time, the Church is not God. If God wants to fill His children with His perfect love, then we cannot look to the Church to fill us. Filling must come from God! The Church can only point someone in the right direction and affirm who God is, but as a Christian one must know God for themselves! Each Christian must fill themselves to experience all of who God is!

Once someone experiences God, then they cannot go through life keeping it all for themselves. If someone is receiving from God but not sharing that with someone else who needs Him, then they are not doing this relationship with God the right way. When God reveals Himself, or blesses someone, it is not just for them. The largest part of what He does *is* for the receiver, but rest assured, it is to be shared with others as well.

Along the same lines, if someone only receives from God at church and is not looking to God to keep themselves filled on their own, they too are not doing this relationship with God the right way. One must grow, much like a baby grows, and eventually go from bottle and spoon feedings to feeding themselves. It may be messy and cute at first, and mistakes and challenges will occur, but if they stick with it, they will become consistent and grow in their relationship with God.

What I am about to say is very important and everyone needs to understand this: *the things of God are continually leaking out of every believer no matter how hard they are holding on to them. There is not a place in our walk with God that allows us to just be filled, without us doing everything it takes to stay filled.* Because we live in a natural body, the things from God's Spirit are leaking out all the time. Our flesh cannot hold all of who God is. Until we get to heaven, our flesh will make sure we must always be filled and filled and filled with God's Spirit and perfect love.

Ephesians 5:18 (NLT) Don't be drunk with wine, because that will ruin your life. Instead, be *filled* with the Holy Spirit.

The words "be filled" mean to live in a constant *state* of being filled. Filled with what? Knowledge of the pastor's super relevant message? The words to the worship band's new song that everyone loves? The coolness of the church's coffee bar? The hipness of a small group leader? The confession to speak over your finances? The mainline truths that a denomination was founded on? The traditional values of our century old church? Whatever a person feels their idea of church is? Emphatically no! The Bible says believers are to live in a state of being filled with the Holy Spirit. This must begin with a knowledge that your relationship is *with God*, not the Church. The moment we replace God with the Church, we are substituting relationship with religion.

I want to ask a question. How can someone be filled with more than they can hold? The answer is quite simple. They can't. If they are to be constantly filled, then that means there must be a leak somewhere. If they are sitting by holding on to what they get at church, they are losing it anyway, whether they know it or not. Why? Because of the leak. I've seen people bounce from church to church because they are looking for that "one service" that fills them so much that they stay "on fire" or "filled with the Spirit" or "good with God" forever. *This scenario does not exist.* The Bible teaches us to fill up with the power and love of God *always*!

Jesus told the disciples in Mark 14:38 when they were sleeping instead of praying with Him, *"Keep watch and pray, so that you will not give in to temptation. For the spirit is willing, but the body is weak."* (NLT)

He was telling them that their spirit man always wants to do what is right, but their body or flesh never wants to do what is right. This is where believers are leaking—*through their flesh.* This doesn't mean we need to wear an absorbent, moisture wicking suit. What that means is, your flesh and your spirit are at odds with one another and the flesh wants what "it" wants and never what the spirit wants. Your flesh is constantly trying to lose spiritual things. Don't believe me? Check yourself the next time you get angry. What's the first thing you think? *Most* of the time it isn't how good God is. That kind of response only comes from years of disciplining your flesh to stay quiet and keeping your spirit full and strong. That means you need to be filled with more of God's Word, God's power, and God's love than you could ever get at church. This may frighten some people because many people's schedules only allow them to attend church once a week. Maybe you don't feel you know enough about God to get yourself filled back up. Don't be afraid of that. You are only *half* of this relationship. *God* wants to keep you filled too. As you grow in your relationship with God, He will be faithful to do His part as well! James 4:8 proves it, *"Come close to God, and God will come close to you."* (NLT)

Since it has been established that we as believers are leaking anyway, why not go ahead and stop being selfish with what God has given us? Share what He says, share what He has done, share what He is doing with others who also need God in their lives! Whatever you know about God or have experienced with God—*no matter how seemingly little or meaningless*—share it with someone else. It doesn't matter if a person doesn't feel adequate or knowledgeable or proficient in the ways of God. People *do* know what God has done *for* and *in* them, and that is all they need to know.

Go make a difference in the world today. When that happens, it makes *more* room for God in your life. This is how you can *stay filled* with more of His goodness again tomorrow. Go ahead and pray for those who are sick. Share Jesus with those who don't know Him. Pray for the big blessing out there beyond your current faith level. Someone may say, "I don't know enough. I haven't been a Christian long enough. I am not a preacher. I can't imagine God blessing me like that." Believers are leaking all those things out every day anyway, but they are also being called to refill those things every day, so go for it!

As I continued to dream, I would see people walk into this "dream church" and most were on empty. No one came in with more than half of a tank. Those at the half mark were few and far between. In the next several pages and chapters, I am going to share what this dream means and how it can affect *your* life! I am thoroughly convinced that we can live a life that *hits the full mark* and experience more of God's goodness, Spirit, and perfect love in our lives. My prayer is that everyone who reads this book—new believer or seasoned saint—learns how to stay full. It all starts with taking the time every day to check the gauges.

Chapter 1

First Things First

Growing up, I was raised in church. I was there as soon as my parents could have me there. It was a small Pentecostal church that was planted and founded by Billy Ray Cyrus' grandfather and Miley Cyrus' great grandfather. Reverend E.L. Cyrus pioneered our church in 1956 in the small town of Flatwoods, Kentucky. I was dedicated to the Lord on Mother's Day, 1971, and I have believed from the beginning that "Jesus loves me.": I sang that song as far back as I can remember, including being in Mrs. Ruth Bradley's Sunday school class for babies.

I have always understood that God's love was on the inside of me because I was taught about Him as a small child. When I began my own relationship with Jesus in 1980 at a youth camp in West Virginia, I began the process of keeping the love of God in my heart on my own. It is so woven into my life now that I don't question it. I believe God loves me and wants to have a relationship with me. Even though over the years

I have done my fair share of things to ruin this relationship, He still loves me.

I ran from God during my senior year at Russell High School until my sophomore year of college. I was going to a University of Kentucky's branch college in my hometown and went on Spring Break with my cousin and two friends to Daytona Beach, Florida. At that time, I was working for a radio station doing disc jockey work and sports casting on the weekend. Without telling the owner or station manager, I took one of the media badges from the news director's office and a tape recorder and headed to Daytona Beach.

"MTV's Spring Break" was in its heyday! My cousin, two of our friends, and I drove my car down to Florida to live it up! It was in this wild week of drinking, pot smoking, LSD tripping, and staying out way too late that God showed me, again, how much He loved me and wanted to have a relationship with me. I spent the week meeting celebrities and MTV's VJs. *(VJs were the announcers and hosts who showed videos on MTV and instead of calling them a DJ or disc jockey, MTV called them video jockeys.)* We had a blast! We came back to the hotel after a morning taping of "Club MTV." I was in the room alone, sitting on the bed, using a beer can for a makeshift marijuana bong. They were sold out of rolling papers all over the city. I was flipping channels on the television, when suddenly, a preacher popped up on the screen and said, "You are going to hell!" Now I don't know what he said before that or to whom he was talking, but right then, I knew he was talking to me. This messed with me, and I didn't have a lot of fun the remainder of the time I was there. We stayed two more days, and then drove back home. I was still shaken from what the minister had said, and as soon as I could, I went to see my pastor.

Pastor Don Adkins is a tall, friendly man who looked like he could've been the lead singer of the country group "Alabama." I was so nervous to talk to him about how I had been living, but he never judged me. He put his arms around me and said, "We're going to make this right today." We talked for some time, and he assured me more than once that God still, despite what I had done wrong, loved me and wanted to have a relationship with me.

He said something I still hear as crystal clear today as I did then. He said, "Make this a quality decision. Make this the one where you really change." He led me in a prayer that changed my life, and I rededicated my life back to Jesus. I have never been the same. I wish I could say that I have been perfect over the years, but that's not true. I've had my fair share of failures. However, in my imperfections I have always believed that God loved me and wanted to further my relationship with Him. That is what kept me getting back up and trying again. I believe God desired to have me close to Him.

Since that time, I have attended and graduated from Bible college, majoring in pastoral ministry. In addition, I attained an Associate's degree in Theology, a Bachelor's degree in Business, and a Doctorate degree in Ministerial Leadership. I married a wonderful girl from California with a strong ministry heritage. I have yet to figure out how I got her. How something that good ended up in my life is a mystery. She is incredible and gifted and beautiful and caring and when she reads this she will be overly happy with me. (LOL!) I love her. I can only scratch my head in amazement at how much God loves me and blessed me by giving her to me.

Jodi and I also have two sons who constantly cause my eyes to be opened to see how much the Father loves us. As much as I love those two, the Bible says, "How much more will your Father in Heaven give good gifts to those who ask Him?" I have a hard time imagining that because I love my boys so much and would do anything to make them happy. It is almost inconceivable to imagine how much He loves me and wants to have a relationship with me. I have not been able to sabotage God's love for me and my relationship with Him is growing greater and greater every day.

Aside from my own personal story, I have *huge* news for you. God wants to have a relationship with you! He wants to fill your heart and mind in a greater way than the people you love can. He wants to be the center of your life. He is very interested in *you.*

God created you uniquely. He added a piece of Himself to you that He has not unleashed in creation until that point! If one thinks back to the story of the Garden of Eden in Genesis, God spent six days creating everything from the heavens and the earth. He created the land, water, stars, the moon, the sun, mountains, trees, continents, animals, rivers, grass, and even Adam. Even after God created all those things there was still a part of Himself that He had not expressed in creation yet. He still had to create a woman. Something that had never been expressed that possessed such beauty was still in God's mind.

Think of everything one can see in creation. Now thanks to things like the Hubble Telescope, we can see and experience so much more of creation. The beauty of the cosmos is breathtaking, and we still cannot capture it all with our minds. We are just now starting to understand that some of what we thought were "stars" are millions of other galaxies with billions of stars inside them. We still have no idea what is inside those galaxies.

There is still undiscovered beauty that God has expressed in creation that we don't know about yet. The views we have here on planet Earth are enough to make your eyes water and your heart skip a beat. These are views of things like the Grand Canyon, Niagara Falls, Bora Bora, Hawaii, Venice, the Alps, and other beautiful places on the earth. Imagine all of creation when it was brand new. How much of God was poured out to make all of that? Even after creating the heavens and the earth, He still expressed Himself in a new way. He created Adam, a perfect man. After creating Adam, He expressed Himself again in a new way by creating Eve. Even though that is mind-boggling, we are not even beginning to scratch the surface.

Here is the big news: *God did the same thing with you.* He did not express Himself in a completely new way until He created you. You are a unique expression of God's creativity. There isn't another person like you! If you want to know how unique you are, just look at your fingerprints. Of the billions and billions of people who have lived and are living on the planet right now, you are the only one who has those fingerprints. He created you uniquely so that you could be full of His goodness and have a loving relationship with Him.

No matter where in the world you were born, no matter into what situation you were born, no matter toward what tendencies you lean, no matter what flaws you have, no matter what strengths you cling to, God is crazy about you. He wants to fill you with His perfect love. This filling process begins with accepting all He has done through His perfect love. It happens when you enter a relationship with Jesus. This decision is what finally makes you able to receive the perfect love with which He wants to fill you with. God wants to speak to you, reveal Himself to you, work in your life, and be God *to you*, *through you*, and *for you*!

As we will discuss in a later chapter, God created everything. However, when He created humans, God did so because He wanted to have children. His sole purpose for creating everything else was so that we would have a place to live and enjoy. But His purpose in creating us was to have a relationship with us. Like any good parent, He put a set of rules in place.

Genesis 2:15–17 (NLT) The Lord God placed the man in the Garden of Eden to tend and watch over it. But the LORD God warned him; "You may freely eat the fruit of every tree in the garden—*except the tree of the knowledge of good and evil. If you eat its fruit, you are sure to die.*"

It was for our benefit that a rule was put into place; but when the rule was broken, something changed in the DNA of every human being. Let's look at part of a Scripture in Romans.

Romans 5:12, 14–21 (NLT) When Adam sinned, sin entered the world. Adam's sin brought death, so death spread to everyone, for everyone sinned. Still, everyone died—from the time of Adam to the time of Moses—even those...who did not disobey an explicit commandment of God, as Adam did... For the sin of this one man, Adam, brought death to many... For Adam's sin led to condemnation... For the sin of this one man, Adam, caused death to rule over many. Yes, Adam's one sin brings condemnation for everyone... Because one person disobeyed God, many became

sinners... So just as sin ruled over all people and brought them to death...

The DNA of every human being ever to be born, changed and became shackled to the debt that is the price of sin. What changed? The flesh God had made, at that time, could contain the life of God so efficiently that the Bible says that is all that clothed Adam and Eve. They were naked and were not ashamed. The original word naked meant to be clothed by the glory of God and nothing else. This glory was the life of God that He breathed into them when He created them. However, Adam and Eve did what God told them not to do. They sinned. Sin is what separates us from God, and that is how we are born, separated from God. This is what God meant when He told Adam and Eve they would die. Their DNA changed because of sin. The life of God that clothed Adam and Eve would have caused them to live forever, physically. But when they sinned, that life began to leak out. This is when they realized they were naked. This word naked here is a different version from the original one. This version of the word naked is the one humanity knows now as to be covered by nothing.

Colossians 2:13 (NLT) *You were dead because of your sins* and because your sinful nature was not yet cut away.

Romans 6:23 (NLT) For the wages of sin is death...

For something to be affected genetically, its blood must be changed. This is exactly what happened to Adam and Eve. Sin changed their blood, which changed their bodies. Their bodies became porous and the life of God began to leak out. Until they broke the rules, their bodies were fully capable of housing the glory and presence of God, which is why they could be in such close contact with Him.

The scripture says they recognized the sound of God walking in the cool of the day. That is the kind of relationship we all wish we had with Him. They could tell it was God by the way His walk sounded. Suddenly, they realized they were naked and became ashamed. That realization meant something had to have happened to their bodies for them to suddenly see themselves so differently. I believe, and it is my opinion, their very blood changed because of their sin, and it caused their bodies to change.

Leviticus 17:11 (NLT) For *the life of the body is in its blood.* I have given you the blood on the altar to purify you, making you right with the Lord. It is the blood given in exchange for a life that makes purification possible.

Changing of the blood does bring about cosmetic changes to the body in an unusual, but common way today. When someone eats too many carrots, their skin will turn orange. *Science Line* at the University of California, Santa Barbara states, "Skin can change colors because of the beta-carotene, a pigment that is present in high amounts. If you eat too much, *the excess beta-carotene enters the bloodstream.* It is not broken down and instead, is deposited in the skin."

Similarly, what happens to someone's skin when their oxygen level in their blood drops? Their skin turns blue. What happens when the liver doesn't metabolize old blood cells the right way? The blood cells leak a yellow pigment called bilirubin and the skin turns yellow or jaundiced.

Adam and Eve's blood changed, so they became carriers for sin, much like carriers for other diseases that are spread in the world today. To give man any chance of life, in a world without Him, God had to shed animal blood, where physical life is found, until He could set things right again.

Genesis 3:21 (NLT) And the Lord God made clothing from animal skins for Adam and his wife.

It was the shedding of blood that allowed Adam and Eve to survive. In a way, it was a blood transfusion. God ordered the shedding of the blood of animals for thousands of years to keep mankind alive so He could restore things and have a relationship with humanity again. Taking the lives of animals became the pattern that kept man in "temporary right-standing" with God. It was a band-aid of sorts.

Jesus became the "donor" God would use to make a permanent blood transfusion so we could be cured from sin. He was brought into the world in much the same way as Adam. God took a lump of lifeless genetic material, (dust of the ground for Adam and an unfertilized egg from the Virgin Mary for Jesus) and breathed life into both. He placed life and blood into a being for the first time. Both Adam and Jesus were born sinless. It's important to say that God's Spirit is what fertilized Mary's egg, not a man. By doing this, Jesus didn't inherit the DNA of sin because it was not transferred through *the blood* like everyone else that had been born.

As Adam and Jesus were both born in the same state, only Jesus finished life the way God wanted all of us to finish life—sinless. When He did this, He could complete the blood transfusion humanity needed. He could offer a whole new blood supply and lifeline. This new blood was guaranteed when He rose from the dead.

When death tried to take the life of Jesus the same way it tried to take the rest of creation, death was unjustified in its actions. Death is only meant to take the life of things that have blood tainted by sin. Jesus had sinless blood. When death tried to take a person's life that it was not allowed to take, Jesus broke death and became its Lord. This is the most important part. Jesus then rose from the dead, and by doing so He restored the order of things to how God had originally intended. Now, Jesus lives forever in Heaven getting a place ready for all who accept Him, and this blood transfusion, by faith.

John 14:3 (NIV) And if I go and prepare a place for you, I will come back and take you with me that you also may be where I am.

This is the reason that when you accept what Jesus did, you are "born again." Before God, you accepted a new bloodline in your spirit, and you are blameless and sinless. *Because of what Jesus did, you are alive!* That means you will live forever. It may not be in this body, as it is, but you will live forever.

John 3:16 (NLT) For this is how God loved the world: He gave his one and only Son, so that everyone who believes in Him will not perish but have *eternal* life.

All this change happens to us, on a spiritual level, as soon as we begin our relationship with Jesus. Your spirit is transformed instantaneously but your flesh begins a lifelong process of change until it is glorified in Heaven. This process is made up of three things that happen to all believers.

First, God looks at you as having been made right or to say it in a "churchy" way, justified. Have you ever been accused of being wrong about something and you tried to justify your actions? You were trying to explain away any guilt so that someone wouldn't think you were wrong. This is what Jesus's death does when you accept what He did. It removes any guilt you have and completely removes any wrong you have in your life. It is done instantly, and you are no longer guilty of the bad things you have done in your life as far as God is concerned.

Romans 4:25 (NIV) He was delivered over to death *for our sins* and was raised to life *for our justification*.

The second thing that happens is you are recreated or "born again." You are not the same person you were before. You are instantly changed on the inside and have become a very different person. You are what the Bible calls a "new creation."

2 Corinthians 5:17 (NLT) If anyone belongs to Christ, He is a new person. The old life is gone; a new life has begun.

Both things are instant changes that happen as soon as you accept Jesus as Lord. One reason Jesus came was to destroy death and, just as He rose from the dead, so will we. Those who accept Jesus will rise from the dead and live forever—this is the way God intended it to be from the very beginning. Eventually, even our bodies will be changed to be the bodies God intended them to be. It is important to understand that even though death is defeated and cannot hold those who accept Jesus forever, it hasn't been destroyed yet. Those who haven't accepted Jesus will still be subject to death's destruction and eternal separation from God forever.

1 Corinthians 15:26 (NLT) The last enemy that will be destroyed is death.

Believer's bodies will die but will not stay dead forever. That is the hope we have in Him. We will live forever with Him!

Here is the first step to filling yourself with the perfect love of God. Accept the fact that Jesus, God's Son, paid your debt, defeated death, and wants you to have a loving relationship with God. What you were born owing, *He already paid.* What you owed, that you didn't even know you owed, has been fully paid. There is no reason for you to keep paying for what you once owed, but could never pay, from of *your* own life. You can now live a life that brings glory to God.

Romans 5:12–20 (NLT) When Adam sinned, sin entered the world. Adam's sin brought death, so death spread to everyone, for everyone sinned. Yes, people sinned even before the law was given. But it was not counted as sin because there was not yet any law to break. Still, everyone died—from the time of Adam to the time of Moses—even those who did not disobey an explicit commandment of God, as Adam did. Now Adam is a symbol, a representation of Christ, who was yet to come. But there is a great difference between Adam's sin and God's gracious gift. For the sin of this one man, Adam, brought death to many. *But even greater is God's wonderful grace and His gift of forgiveness to many through this other man, Jesus Christ.* And the result of God's gracious gift is very different from the result of that one man's sin. For Adam's sin led to condemnation, but *God's free*

gift leads to our being made right with God, even though we are guilty of many sins. **For the sin of this one man, Adam, caused death to rule over many. But even greater is** ***God's wonderful grace and His gift of righteousness, for all who receive it will live in triumph over sin and death through this one man, Jesus Christ.*** **Yes, Adam's one sin brings condemnation for everyone,** ***but Christ's one act of righteousness brings a right relationship with God and new life for everyone.*** **Because one person disobeyed God, many became sinners.** ***But because one other person obeyed God, many will be made righteous.*** **God's law was given so that all people could see how sinful they were. But as people sinned more and more, God's wonderful grace became more abundant. So just as sin ruled over all people and brought them to death, now** ***God's wonderful grace rules instead, giving us right standing with God and resulting in eternal life through Jesus Christ our Lord.***

Jesus did all of this to have a relationship with you. You are His unique creation. You are a specific piece of Himself that He made to live now, in this time and space. Deep down, we all have that desire toward spiritual things. This desire is what causes us to find God, experience God, and become children of God as He desires.

The third thing that happens when we accept Jesus is we enter the process that this book is meant to address. It is the *process* of "sanctification." Sanctification is a big, scary church word that is something we all are living out right now. *Sanctification is the life-long process of changing the outward man to become what the inward man has already been changed to instantaneously.* This process is one that will take your whole life. Those who do not *live the sanctified part of salvation* are not experiencing the *full benefit* of salvation. People need to see you change because if you don't, there will be no evidence in your life that God is real.

Hebrews 12:14 (NIV) Make every effort to live in peace with everyone and to be *holy*; without holiness no one will see the Lord.

The first two things that happen when you accept Jesus are the most important because they allow you to have a relationship with God. The third element of salvation is also very important. This verse in Hebrews doesn't mean that without complete holiness nobody will ever see God. What is holiness? It's the evidence that sanctification is happening. The changing of the outside man to be more like the inside man produces holiness and our lives start to show it. Complete holiness is what we are striving towards but nobody has achieved it yet. But we should still strive to be holy because if we are not, how can anyone see God in us?

If God did all of this for you to have a relationship with you, we should do everything we are supposed to do to keep this relationship fresh and full of His goodness. Then and only then can we grow in our walk with Him. Therefore, others will see Him in us too!

Remember we are leaking, and if we don't fill ourselves back up with His goodness, we won't stay full. Our relationship with Him will start to drain and not be what it's supposed to be. If we allow the process to go on too long, our relationship with God may become non-existent. So, the big question we are addressing in this book is this: *How do we go about keeping our relationship with God as full as possible?* Let's start putting some fuel in this tank!

The First Quarter of the Tank: Read Your Bible

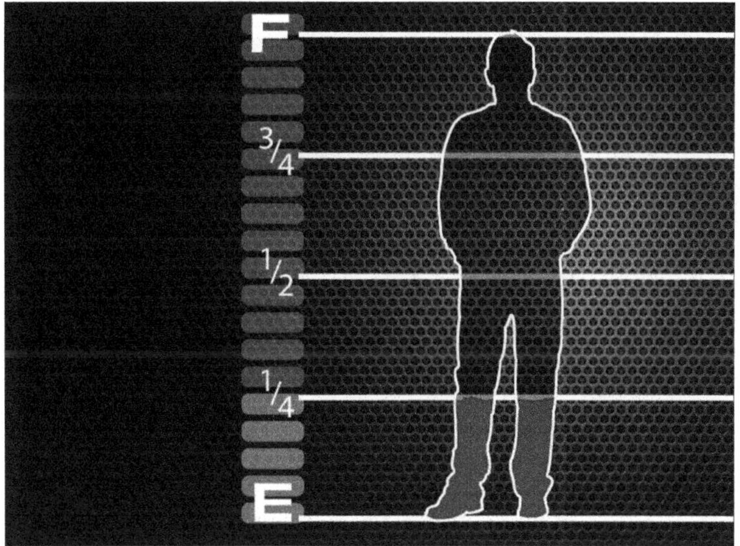

Chapter 2

Read Your Bible

I spent more than the first two decades of my ministry career as a full-time youth pastor. I loved every second of it, and I still speak at youth conferences, camps, and retreats. I am convinced I will always be part of youth ministry. In those 20 plus years with teenagers, I cannot tell you how many messages I delivered with a key to a successful Christian walk being "Read your Bible and pray!" This has been a staple for all youth pastors everywhere for decades. There have been worship songs that have lyrics that read, "I will read my Bible and pray."

This is a testament and snapshot of the message of youth ministry. But to be a successful Christian in any age of life, you must read your Bible and pray. Sadly, it hasn't been said enough to enough people, because our churches and even Bible colleges are full of people with no basic knowledge of the Bible. There have been times when I have been teaching and I have said, "You know when Daniel stood in front of the lion in the lion's den," and I've had people look at me like they had no idea what I was talking about. *The Bible is the foundation of our Christian life and needs to be the first thing we put in our life.* Input of the Word will fill us with God's goodness and put us on the path to achieving the full Christian life.

I cherish having been raised in Sunday school and learning Bible stories. These cute little stories that were often told with a pale blue felt board and dramatically drawn pictures of the Bible characters. They have become the solid foundation for my life. I didn't grow up listening to these stories as fairy tales. I grew up hearing these Bible stories as examples of how God can and will move in my life.

The reality of the Bible is not something that can just be studied like a textbook and obtained. As a kid, I remember diving over desks to catch candy for the right answer to the Bible quiz at the end of the lesson. I remember quoting back memory verses every week. I had the Word fed to me as far back as I can remember. In all those fun times as a kid in Sunday school, I would get in trouble for talking too loud, making the teacher upset because I leaned my seat against the wall, or chewing gum and blowing bubbles loudly and obnoxiously.

Despite all of that, I can confidently say that the Word was getting inside me. There are so many times I faced a challenge that was very scary, a problem so big it looked like it would take me out, or an issue that looked too big to do anything about. In the face of every one of those, a scripture I learned as a kid or in youth group came from my heart and I would speak it out of my mouth. It may have even been one I hadn't thought about since 1983 in Rita Robinson's Vacation Bible School class, or 1985 when my Uncle Dwight or cousin Todd (both in ministry now) as my youth ministers drilled it into my head. Even my mom and dad took a turn at teaching my class and those foundations from the Word came up all of the time. Knowing God's Word is a treasure chest that keeps paying, even today.

When my son Preston was born, we were at the hospital and things didn't look like they would work out for us. Preston and his younger brother Peyton were both adopted from birth. The first experience with adoption was a mountain-sized challenge for us. We had been at the hospital and bonded with him when suddenly we started getting reports that Preston would not be going home with us. Our world was caving in all around us.

We had tried to get pregnant using every method and trick conveyed to us as well as the traditional way. We also tried in vitro, artificial insemination, eating fists full of vitamins, eating different foods, urinating on sticks to measure optimum fertility periods, sitting on ice packs, changing the kind of undergarment, watching the moon cycle, and the list goes on and on and, to be honest, we are now so glad that none of those worked. God blessed us with the two greatest gifts we could have ever been given.

Meanwhile, back in the hospital, we had the goal of a baby within our grasp. The end to this long struggle to have children seemed to be ending. When suddenly this precious gift looked like he was being ripped from our hands at the last minute. I remember feeling like I had been punched in the stomach. My dad regularly calls me "Spock" because he says I don't cry. But on my thirty-sixth birthday, I cried more than I had in years.

Preston was born on February 19th, the day before my birthday. I couldn't believe this beautiful baby boy God blessed us with was going to be taken away from us. I remember crying out to God about how this whole thing had transpired.

A girl who managed the crisis pregnancy center was a former student of mine when I was an instructor at Bible college. The short version of the story is we spoke briefly about Jodi and I being interested in exploring options for adoption. Nine months later, she called and asked me if I was still interested in adoption. She knew a young expecting mother from the pregnancy center who was looking to give her baby up for adoption. We were thrilled and answered with a resounding "Yes!"

Three months later, here we were at the hospital, having our hearts broken. During this life-changing challenge that seemed to be ruining the happiest day since our marriage, a scripture came up from inside me. It was Psalm 37:23, "*The steps of a good man are ordered by the Lord: and he delights in his way.*" (NKJV)

I hadn't thought of that scripture, in and of itself, in years, but there it was, coming up from the inside. That verse had been placed there and forgotten about. I changed what I believed from worrying to embracing the fact that God didn't bring us all the way there to jerk the rug out from under our feet. After all, He had directed our steps to this point. I believed He was going to take delight in what happened, and He wouldn't delight in our misery.

To show the power and stability of God's Word in the shortest way possible, let me just say that everything worked out and God directed every step of the process to ensure that Preston was and is ours. As I write this book, he is eight years old and loves video games, tae-kwon-do, animals, (especially the million lizards we have in Florida) and is an honor roll student on his report card. He and his brother have brought so much joy to our lives, and it was a total reliance on God's Word that made it happen! Everything in the Word is meant to help us in our lives today!

No matter how we were raised or what background we may come from, when we put the Word of God inside of us, we are on our way to living the full Christian life the way God intended. I was fortunate to have had it there as a child, but many people are not that fortunate. The good news is that you can change that. The Word of God doesn't have a shelf life, meaning it doesn't expire or go stale. It's always going to be good. However, the Word must be partaken of. The Word will only work if we start putting it in our hearts. God's Word will make a huge difference in our life whenever we begin to accept it.

I believe we are obligated to take the time to tell people what the Bible says instead of assuming they know it or have heard it. However, what about the people who have been coming to church for years and still don't have a basic knowledge of the Bible, Bible stories, foundational scriptures, and more? There is an old song from the 1980s and the words were so elementary that they are worth sharing now: "Get in the Word and the Word will get in you." The Apostle Peter hammered this point when he tells us the Word will cause growth in our relationship with God.

1 Peter 2:2–3 (NLT) Like newborn babies, you must crave pure spiritual milk (the King James Version reads, "sincere milk of the

Word") **so that you will grow into a full experience of salvation. Cry out for this nourishment, now that you have had a taste of the Lord's kindness.**

Therefore, our first quarter of a tank in our quest to living filled is the input of the Word of God. There is nothing more important as a Christian than reading the Bible. Every word that's in the Bible is a word we believe God said. Even though all of God's Word must be received by faith, there is no guesswork in what is in the Scripture. It is right there in black and white. If we will dare to apply everything we find in scripture, our lives as believers begin to fill.

Chapter 3

Why Is the Bible First?

Today, humanity replaces everything. If something is broken, worn out, or sometimes even dirty, it is discarded and replaced with something brand new. There are stories of perfectly good earth-moving machines being left inside coal mines that are still in working order simply because it's too much work to get them out and it may be cheaper for the company to leave them there.

Generations before saved everything even if it was broken. To this day, my parents still have the first set of worn out tires from my 1987 Firebird in their attic. These tires are bald and have the steal belts hanging out of them. Why did them keep them? Maybe it's for sentimental reasons. Perhaps they kept them to serve as a reminder for me to drive slower. Who knows? An emergency may arise where an old set of dry rotted tires may come in handy.

I believe my parents picked up this behavior from their parents, who both lived through the Great Depression. In those days, to have anything—no matter how old or what condition it was in—was a big deal. That generation didn't know when they were going to get anything again so they kept everything. This behavior was passed down to their children and then on to my generation. As I look around my house, I have a plethora of things that belonged to both sets of my grandparents. I have learned to hang on to a lot of things, also.

Today, things are so much different. The life expectancy of something is not what it used to be. A five-year-old computer is almost worthy of a museum. My iPhone has more computing power than the first computer I ever received in 1994. That same iPhone has more computing power than all of NASA had in 1969 when it placed two astronauts on the moon.

As a child of the 80s, I had an Atari 2600. I spent hours playing it in fourth and fifth grade. I still have mine, and it still works. I got it out one night and plugged it into our big screen television. Preston, who was three at the time was ready to turn it off in just a matter of minutes. Of course, he was comparing it to his "Xbox 360" which has 16,384 times the processing power of my old Atari.

This is the attitude of today: things are outdated in months. How many software updates does a phone alone do in one year? Things are completely obsolete in a few years. How many times has someone had to buy the newest version of a software package because the company doesn't service the last one anymore? The thought of a decade becomes ancient history.

It is in this concept I want to present the first one-quarter tank. Society has started to explain away the Bible as being archaic and irrelevant because some parts of it are over 3,000 years old. That is somewhat difficult for people to wrap their minds around. The Bible, in parts, is three and a half millennia old.

The Latin word for millennia, in my opinion, refers to the length of time that passes when I rode cross country with my family—from Kentucky to California and back—in a 1983 Chevy van. While this trip was dragging by, my cousin and I were aggravating the daylights out of the each other. There was no television. There was no iPad. There was no flip down movie screen. There was only "car bingo" and "license plate alphabet search" and of course "slug bug." This is what a millennium is, or at least that's what it seemed like it.

In sincerity, a millennium is 1,000 years. In looking at part of the Bible being three and a half of those old, we must ask ourselves, "How can something so old have any relevance today?"

Many say that the Bible cannot be relevant today. They say that the Bible is like an Atari. It was useful and fun for a while but now the Bible is an outdated relic of the good-old days. In some people's opinion, "Society has changed and so has what defines right and wrong." It's funny—well, sad really—that in the middle of doing their part to discredit the Bible, many of these "experts" are experiencing loveless marriages that are falling apart because of selfishness. People that were in their circle of friends are consistently changing because they are stabbing each other in the back instead of building true and life-long friendships. Sexually transmitted diseases and substance abuse show their effects on their bodies. Many are suffering from credit card debt that swallows their bank account while they themselves are self-destructing. Of course, the Bible isn't true in their lives. But the question is, "Are they attempting to make it true?"

The argument of the Bible's relevance does make sense from a purely humanistic point of view. Sure, everything changes, doesn't it? Over time, values change. What was considered appropriate dress in the 1920s would probably land you in the HR office getting written up today—or at the very least get you a lot of strange looks. A Model T will not get you very far on the interstate today. Of course, the things that needed to change such as women's rights and civil rights were a wonderful awakening and abolishment of ignorance.

There has been and always will be growth in mankind. What we know and discover will cause us to change. However, regardless of what we know, what is true will never change. Truth is not a constantly changing idea. It is not a fashion statement or something that can be explained away. It is not changed or altered by time or by culture. Truth is truth no matter what we feel about it.

There are plenty of things you may not like about math, but no matter what anyone else tries to tell you, two plus two will always equal four. It doesn't matter how much you try to say it's three or five, the truth is, two plus two is four.

Regardless of what you think about gravity, it still holds you on the earth. It is irrelevant if you believe in gravity or not, that physical law will always exist. If the physical laws of this life are unchanging, then why would the spiritual laws, that created the physical laws be any different?

God's Word Created Everything

What better place to go than the beginning? It will help us see the importance of the input of God's Word if we understand this—*the Word of God created everything.* Everything ever created began as a Word coming out of God's mouth. No smoke, no mirrors, no waiving His hands. He just said it and it happened.

Genesis 1:1–31 (NIV) In the beginning God created the heavens and the earth. Now the earth was formless and empty, darkness was over the surface of the deep, and the Spirit of God was hovering over the waters. *And God said,* "Let there be light," and there was light. God saw that the light was good, and he separated the light from the darkness. *God called* the light "day," and the *darkness he called* "night." And there was evening, and there was morning—the first day. *And God said,* "Let there be a vault between the waters to separate water from water." So God made the vault and separated the water under the vault from the water above it. And it was so. *God called* the vault "sky." And there was evening, and there was morning—the second day. *And God said,* "Let the water under the sky be gathered to one place, and let dry ground appear." And it was so. *God called* the dry ground "land," and the gathered waters *he called* "seas." And God saw that it was good. *Then God said,* "Let the land produce vegetation: seed-bearing plants and trees on the land that bear fruit with seed in it, according to their various kinds." And it was so. The land produced vegetation: plants bearing seed according to their kinds and trees bearing fruit with seed in it according to their kinds. And God saw that it was good. And there was evening, and there was morning—the third day. *And God said,*

"Let there be lights in the vault of the sky to separate the day from the night, and let them serve as signs to mark sacred times, and days and years, and let them be lights in the vault of the sky to give light on the earth." And it was so. God made two great lights—the greater light to govern the day and the lesser light to govern the night. He also made the stars. God set them in the vault of the sky to give light on the earth, to govern the day and the night, and to separate light from darkness. And God saw that it was good. And there was evening, and there was morning—the fourth day. *And God said* "Let the water teem with living creatures, and let birds fly above the earth across the vault of the sky." So God created the great creatures of the sea and every living thing with which the water teems and that moves about in it, according to their kinds, and every winged bird according to its kind. And God saw that it was good. God blessed them *and said*, "Be fruitful and increase in number and fill the water in the seas, and let the birds increase on the earth." And there was evening, and there was morning—the fifth day. *And God said*, "Let the land produce living creatures according to their kinds: the livestock, the creatures that move along the ground, and the wild animals, each according to its kind." And it was so. God made the wild animals according to their kinds, the livestock according to their kinds, and all the creatures that move along the ground according to their kinds. And God saw that it was good. *Then God said*, "Let us make mankind in our image, in our likeness, so that they may rule over the fish in the sea and the birds in the sky, over the livestock and all the wild animals, and over all the creatures that move along the ground." So God created mankind in his own image, in the image of God he created them; male and female he created

them. God blessed them *and said* to them, "Be fruitful and increase in number; fill the earth and subdue it. Rule over the fish in the sea and the birds in the sky and over every living creature that moves on the ground." *Then God said*, "I give you every seed-bearing plant on the face of the whole earth and every tree that has fruit with seed in it. They will be yours for food. And to all the beasts of the earth and all the birds in the sky and all the creatures that move along the ground—everything that has the breath of life in it—I give every green plant for food." And it was so. God saw all that he had made, and it was very good. And there was evening, and there was morning—the sixth day."

In these verses, we see time after time after time these words: "God said" and "He called." It wasn't until He spoke them out, were those things created. Things didn't function even after they were created by His voice until He called it what it was or told it to "Do this" or "Be this."

In all of this speaking to create, what do you think God was saying? There is only one thing God can say. God always speaks His Word. This doesn't mean that God only quotes the Bible. The Bible is what we *know* God said because it was written down, but everything God speaks, *is* His Word, because it comes from His mind and mouth. If God speaks to you and gives you a word for your life, it *is* His word He speaks to you.

What He speaks to a person's heart may not be an exact quote from the Bible, but it will function in perfect harmony with the Bible because *both* are God's words. God only speaks His Word. Why? Because He is the One to whom those words belong.

If you speak to someone, you are speaking your word. When you try to convince someone that you will do what you said you would do, you might say, "I give you my word." When you give your word, you're putting your integrity and character on the line by saying you will do it. I understand that sometimes we, in our limited humanity, can't do everything we say we will do.

However, if you realize the value in giving your word, you will move heaven and earth and sacrifice many things to make sure you do what you promised. You'll perform the task, even if the original agreement *should* be altered.

I've been the guy who was going to meet someone and got stuck in traffic. (Orlando traffic can be brutal.) I've also been the guy who has had sick kids, a double booking, overslept, flat tires, and the list of excuses can go on and on. But I'm not talking about having to change because a situation caused a real challenge. I'm talking about choosing to change because of not feeling like it or wishing you hadn't committed.

This happens way too often and many have put this characteristic on God. I have not felt like doing something I agreed to do. I have regretted saying I would do it, but I did it anyway because I know my reputation and integrity were on the line. I have also been the one who has made promises to people and have had to sacrifice sleep, time with my family, taken time from work, juggled schedules, taken red-eye flights all night, or some other grand gesture to make sure my word was kept.

This is what God has done for everyone. Humanity has done everything it can to not have a relationship with God, but God is still standing by His Word because He is bound by His own integrity. It is impossible for Him to say anything but His Word and His words are what created everything. By giving creation His Word first He put His integrity and character on the line. His Word was and still is true!

How can you be sure it is still true? Look around. Look up at the sky, breath in the air, smell the flowers, or better yet pinch an arm. How can you pinch yourself and not feel it? We can know God's Word is true because we are here along with all His creation and they are alive. If His Word wasn't true nothing would be here, including us.

The amazing thing is He created everyone to have a relationship and spend time with Him. He created everything else so everyone would have a perfect place to live and enjoy. Just like everyone else, God had a moment when His reputation and integrity were put on the line. His plan was put into jeopardy because the people He created were not able to have that relationship with Him any longer. (This was because of Adam's sin, which took the entire human race out of relationship with God.)

God's integrity and reputation moved heaven and earth and made the ultimate sacrifice to make sure He could have a relationship with everyone! That is why His words created everything. When there were changes that could have completely ended everything He created, the Creator didn't bail out. Who are we to think God couldn't have just destroyed the whole thing? He could have wiped the slate clean, ended all of creation, and started over. The incredible thing about God is He kept His Word when He said, "Let there be." *All of creation still existing is evidence of His Word* and the hope He had that everyone could be restored and have that relationship with Him again. God's Word is the starting point because it made everything.

Hebrews 11:3 (NKJV)...through faith we understand that the worlds were *framed by the word of God*, so that things, which are seen, were not made of things, which do appear.

The Word of God is the very basis for all creation and life. Everything was made from His words. If we could put on a pair of spiritual x-ray goggles and see what everything in this world looks like underneath the surface—past the physical inner workings, past the subatomic quantum world, all the way to the spiritual world—we would see God's words at the very core of everything.

I'm a big movie buff, and if we could see all of creation from God's view, it would be like that scene at the end of the movie *The Matrix*. If you haven't seen this movie, you might have no idea what I am talking about. (It's about a futuristic world where humans have been, unknowingly, enslaved by machines. The body heat of all humans gives the machines the power they need to operate. To keep humanity enslaved and producing body heat, the machines raise them like crops and then put them, from birth, in a dream like state where their very dreams are controlled in a false reality and computer-generated world called "the matrix." [I know, creepy, right?])

On a grander scale, it's an allegory of what has happened to us. Even though the humans are unknowingly in captivity, inside the matrix, they are living their everyday lives going to work or school just like nothing is wrong. The main character, Neo, has a mission to set all of humanity free. He is fulfilling a prophecy, which said a man would be born within the matrix and could change the matrix and free humanity.

Besides having an obvious Messianic allegory through all of humanity being set free, this film also gives us a glimpse of God's Word. Toward the end of the film, from within the matrix, Neo begins to see this computer-generated world for what it is. Instead of dry wall and carpet and bricks and mortar, he sees actual computer code in the shape of walls and flooring. Instead of the villain, he sees computer code making up the shape of the villain. *He begins to see computer code instead of things*. This is much like what we would see behind the veil of reality into the spiritual world. We would see God's words. They are the building blocks for all of creation.

The first reason reading the Bible is so important is because the Word of God created everything. The Bible is God's Word written down, so we can always reference it. Because God's Word is what made everything, then God's Word is also what can change everything, both around and in us.

God's Word Is Perfect

The Word of God is also perfect. The goal of any Christian is to grow and become mature in their relationship with God.

If that is our goal, then what better tool could we put in our hearts than that which is already perfect—the Word of God? We can't become mature if we are not putting something flawless in our hearts. Many Christians have tried to build their relationships with Him on a romanticized idea of who God is and what characteristics God has based solely on what they have heard from someone else. Without the perfection of the Word that came straight from God's mouth, it is impossible for them to become a full Christian.

I completely admit and understand it is very intimidating to measure up to something that is perfect. It's not just intimidating, but it can also be depressing. Many believers will measure their life next to the life of someone who has been walking with Jesus for years or decades and expect to be just like them.

It's even more intimidating when you read the Bible. The characters in the Bible did so much for God and knew God in such a personal way. In the light of those two comparisons, we could easily want to give up because of the stark differences that are seen. Someone once said, "Don't compare someone else's twenty-fifth year with your first." This is what is so great about the perfection found in the Word. The Word does not merely show each person who reads it how lost and messed up their life is. *This perfect Word shows and instructs each us on how to grow and become mature.*

The news gets even better! *The same perfect Word also offers grace and help to cover the shortcomings in our lives which allows us to enjoy the blessings found in the Word while we are growing.* This is what a perfect Word can do.

Proverbs 30:5 (NIV) Every word of God is flawless; he is a shield to those who take refuge in him.

There has been a lot of controversy over the topic of God's Word being perfect. Secular religious "experts" have addressed the Bible as having mistakes in it and contradicting itself. Christian artists and some post-modern ministers have been saying certain things that are stated in the Bible probably never happened. These experts and artists have tried to analyze a perfect book, written by a perfect being, with their imperfect and natural human mind and intellect. Of course, things in the Bible wouldn't make sense to someone thinking solely or mostly from a secular point of view.

You can't fully understand the Word of God with human understanding alone. There is a greater dimension from which the Word of God is written. The only way to understand and fully grasp it is by faith. Again, faith does not do very much for human reasoning.

Human reasoning begins to ask questions like: How does a Creator allow his beloved children to fall out of fellowship with Him? How does a Creator that is all-powerful, allow those children to suffer and allow so much death and pain into the world? How can all of creation spring forth from nothing and be built in six days? How can it rain and flood the whole earth? How can a loving Creator condone slavery in His book? How can a sea part and then collapse back on the enemy? How can a pillar of fire and a pillar of cloud lead three million people around the desert for 40 years? How did that same cloud not lead them any better than being lost for 40 years? How can a man live inside the belly of a giant fish for three days? How can a man be so strong that he kills thousands of the enemy with the jaw-bone of a donkey? How can a shepherd boy kill a military champion who happens to be a giant? How can prophets see amazing visions of the coming Savior? How can God's Son come to earth, never sin, die brutally, and rise from the dead? How can the Holy Spirit fill people and cause people to see a flame of fire over their heads as well as hear these same people, who are from another country, speak their language perfectly, with no accent, and in their own dialect, all while they are declaring the goodness of God? How can the world end with the Second Coming of the Savior and all hell breaks loose?

Isn't all this a little over the top and a little fantastic? Isn't this just crazy talk? I mean, isn't this just a little weird? From a completely natural point of view the answer is a resounding "Yes!' These things sound like make-believe stories and are full of content that makes great movies. But God is so much broader and deeper than any human understanding.

Isaiah 55:8 (NLT) "My thoughts are nothing like your thoughts," says the LORD. "And my ways are far beyond anything you could imagine."

What if for one second you were to accept these stories as more than fairy tales and accepted them as truth? What if you dared to believe them as examples of how God can and wants to move in your life? When you do, these stories that seemed to be so fantastic and unbelievable begin to take on a whole new meaning and relevance to your life and what you're going through currently. These perfect words start to do their job.

I don't claim to be an "expert" that has achieved the level of the talking heads on the big news channels or politically-themed talk shows. And I don't claim to be a hip Christian artist that has a following of tens of thousands, or a post-modern pastor with a congregation of thousands and multiple off-site campuses. Despite all that, allow me to ask some questions.

What if everything God said was perfect and those Words were always perfect in the middle of the imperfect situation? What if that imperfect situation was a product from the choices that human beings made while rejecting those perfect words? What if all the spectacular stories did happen exactly as told? What if the further we, as humanity, go along in time, we are allowing ourselves to believe in the power of God less and less because *we* are not expecting Him to show His power like He once did?

There are things that happened years ago that I don't recollect as I did when it first happened. Most do not remember being a newborn baby. Think about it this way—I want you to remember back as far as you can. How far back can you go? First grade? Kindergarten? Pre-school? I can make it back to about three years old.

I remember being in the nursery class at church and singing kids songs with my nursery teacher. I have some flashes of when I was two years old, but that is because I was in the hospital with pneumonia, and it was very traumatic. I don't have clear memories of that though. How far did you make it?

Most people don't remember past three years of age. This is due to what psychologists call "childhood amnesia." Scientists have discovered that by the age of six or seven, things that happened at three are still very vivid in a child's memory. But as they turn eight or nine, they tend to lose up to 60 percent of the memory they had just a year or two before.

The point I want to make is this: just because you can't remember all the way back to the time you were born doesn't mean that your birth didn't happen, does it? As we travel through time, we are thousands of years removed from the time Jesus walked the earth, turning water into wine, raising Lazarus from the dead, walking on the water, the pouring out of the Holy Spirit, the miracles performed by the Apostles, and so on. As the population increases and people who have never heard about Jesus yet are born, it is easy to explain away the stories and perfection of the Bible as imperfect and fairy tales because those stories are being passed down from generation to generation.

Over time, our reasoning and thinking have become less familiar with anything being that spectacular. Sadly, people's thoughts are being replaced with science and technology and what man can do on his own. There have been scientists who theorize things didn't happen that way. *By accepting theories as absolute truth, isn't humanity putting more faith in men than God?* These men, who are incredibly smart and intelligent, are no closer to proving their theories. At the end of their documentaries and books, they will also say, "This is how *I believe* it happened." It is an act of faith for them as well.

Has humanity come to think so highly of itself that the most educated human being can completely understand how all this began? These people summarize that these amazing events cannot be true and when asked why, they will not respond with evidence, but rather with theories. When asked about creation and what the Bible says, these people usually say, "The Bible contradicts itself, so it can't be true." But what if, in fact, it is true?

As we discussed earlier, from the time of creation, God told Adam and Eve that *if* they were to eat of the tree of the knowledge of good and evil, they would surely die.

Gen 2:15–17 (NLT) The Lord God placed the man in the Garden of Eden to tend and watch over it. But the Lord God warned him;

"You may freely eat the fruit of every tree in the garden—*except the tree of the knowledge of good and evil. If you eat its fruit, you are sure to die.*"

Some people will read that verse from Genesis and say, "Why give humans any choice? Just make everything automatic." That over-simplification does serve their argument. However, the argument does not make sense when it comes to a living relationship with a living person.

From a purely humanistic point of view, no choice fixes the problem. However, a relationship with a living God is what mankind is attempting to achieve. Would anyone want love to be automatic? If you are in a relationship with someone, do you want them to love you because they "*have to*" or because they *choose* to? Why would God want anything less? God came up with a plan to restore that relationship as soon as it was broken. He wanted His words to ring true forever.

This next statement may rattle your idea of what was going on here. God didn't threaten Adam and Eve with immediate death. The words "die" in the story of Genesis do not mean cease to exist immediately. God was not threatening His children to force them to obey. God was warning Adam and Eve what would happen.

The forbidden fruit was not poisonous. God was addressing a larger problem that comes from people not obeying what He told them to do. The word die means Adam and Eve would be separated from God—that He could not spend time with them, like He had, anymore. Think about that. The Bible says God walked on the earth in the cool of the day. He did this so frequently that Adam and Eve recognized the way His walk sounded. That happened regularly. God would literally come down to earth and hang out with Adam and Eve.

When He told them they would die, that meant they would die spiritually. Adam and Eve's flesh would become like a grandfather clock and eventually wind down and die. His word to them was perfect. He gave them a choice to love Him. His perfect words should have been more important than any other influence. It was Adam and Eve who decided otherwise. Adam and Eve's choice brought about the unleashing of sin and death on the world. This is where murder, slavery, human trafficking, sickness, terrorism, divorce, addiction, depression, and any type of evil and bad things came from. This evil now had freedom to run wild over all humanity—from the choices of the first two human beings.

Romans 5:12, 14–19, 21 (NLT) "When Adam sinned, sin entered the world. Adam's sin brought death, so death spread to everyone, for everyone sinned… Still, everyone died—from the time of Adam to the time of Moses—even those who did not disobey an explicit commandment of God, as Adam did. For the sin of this one man, Adam, brought death to many … for Adam's sin led to condemnation … For the sin of this one man, Adam, caused death to rule over many… Yes, Adam's one sin brings condemnation for everyone … Because one person disobeyed God, many became sinners… So just as sin ruled over all people and brought them to death.

God did not create humans to be robots who *must* serve Him. He created children with a free will to serve Him because they *choose* to serve Him. He gave perfect words that had conditions and consequences. Throughout the Word we see God referred to as Father. When parents have children, some of the most frustrating times of parenting are when the child exercises their free will. Even though it causes the hair to go grey, it's the free will of the child and those choices that make the love parents feel towards their children (or even the love people feel for one another) grow deeper and richer. It is those character traits that come from free will that cause the love of those people, as they are, to be enriched. It is then that we *want* to love them, not *have* to love them.

In my career as a youth pastor, I saw many teenagers who refused to follow exactly what their parents wanted them to do. They chose otherwise as soon as they were old enough to make their own choices. They root for different sports teams. (Imagine lifelong Yankee fans raising kids that end up rooting for the Red Sox. Or Ohio State Buckeye fans' kids rooting for Michigan. Or Kentucky fans' rooting for Louisville!) The kids vote different politically, such as republicans producing democratic children. They date the "wrong kind of people" as when the good girl brings home the bad boy, and so on.

However, once the children realize the value of the wisdom and love their parents *did* give them, their relationships usually grow. Adults will remember the first time something their parents used to do that seemed so stupid to them as a teenager, made complete sense to them as an adult. That realization about their parents usually makes them feel very humble. At that time, their love and appreciation for their parents increased.

Likewise, parents will remember the first time their child started to make decisions on their own, like the first time they cleaned their room on their own. The first time they said, "I love you, Mommy or Daddy" on their own. The first time they did their homework without being made to. The first time they came home on time. These moments were such a satisfying feeling because the child started to show love and respect without being *made* to do so. It became both child and parent loving each other equally and appreciating each other. This is a product of free will.

This is the same thing that happened with Adam and Eve. God's perfect words of creation and perfect words of consequence made the way possible for everyone to have a deeper and more intimate relationship with Him because they can choose that relationship! That is the positive side of free will. However, Adam and Eve didn't use free will to increase their relationship with God. They chose not to take God at His word and that came with consequences. It's sad too because God's words were perfect from the beginning.

When it comes to bad things that happen in the world, God, in His goodness, gave perfect words. These words were not to condone bad things but to give advice to people so that *all* would have a chance at experiencing goodness in their lives. But when sin entered the world, Satan was given control of everything on the earth and the way man did things started becoming less and less like God.

2 Corinthians 4:4 (NLT) Satan, *who is the god of this world*, has blinded the minds of those who don't believe. They are unable to see the glorious light of the Good News. They don't understand this message about the glory of Christ, who is the exact likeness of God.

With things being the way man's choices caused them to be, God gave perfect words to people in every kind of horrible situation that you could think of. These perfect words would cause them to have as good a life as possible, *until God could fix everything*. God never said bad things like slavery, abuse, and everything else bad, was acceptable. He was saying that despite the fact human beings, under the influence of Satan, have created and practiced horrible things, there is a way to have tolerable (at least as tolerable as it could be) and peaceful times in their lives. These statements were, once again, band-aids until He could set things right. He did set things right, when Jesus came, died, rose again, and became Lord. He came to set the world back to the standard of the perfect Word from which God created it.

Romans 5:12–20 (NLT) When Adam sinned, sin entered the world. Adam's sin brought death, so death spread to everyone, for everyone sinned. Yes, people sinned even before the law was given. But it was not counted as sin because there was not yet any law to break. Still, everyone died—from the time of Adam to the time of Moses—even those who did not disobey an explicit commandment of God, as Adam did. Now Adam is a symbol, a representation of Christ, who was yet to come. But there is a great difference between Adam's sin and God's gracious gift. For the sin of this one man, Adam, brought death to many. ***But even greater is God's wonderful grace and his gift of forgiveness to many through this other man, Jesus Christ.*** **And the result of God's gracious gift is very different from the result of that one man's sin. For Adam's sin led to condemnation, but** ***God's gift leads to our being made right with God, even though we are guilty of many sins.*** **For the sin of this one man, Adam, caused death to rule over many. But even greater is** ***God's wonderful grace and his gift of righteousness, for all who receive it will live in triumph over sin and death through this one man, Jesus Christ.*** **Yes, Adam's one sin brings condemnation for everyone,** ***but Christ's one act of righteousness***

brings a right relationship with God and new life for everyone.* Because one person disobeyed God, many became sinners. *But because one other person obeyed God, many will be made righteous.* God's law was given so that all people could see how sinful they were. But as people sinned more and more, God's wonderful grace became more abundant. So just as sin ruled over all people and brought them to death, now *God's wonderful grace rules instead, giving us right standing with God and resulting in eternal life through Jesus Christ our Lord.

If Jesus came to set the world back to the standard of the perfect Word from which God created it, then the only way those who have accepted Jesus can enjoy it, is to find out what that perfect Word says.

God's Word is perfect in all things. Human actions are what made creation imperfect through the releasing of sin and death. Humanity's actions twisted and perverted God's perfection. People's actions started the process that led to things becoming imperfect. People were, and still are flawed. Until we accept what the only perfect person—Jesus—did for us, we will stay flawed. *Those who have a relationship with Jesus come back in contact with God and can begin to understand that which is perfect, God's Word, again.* God's Word is perfect and once we accept it as perfect, believe it, and see it through faith, we can expect this perfect Word to change our world.

God's Word Is Limitless in Power

Not only is the Word the basis for everything in creation and perfect, but it is also limitless in its power. We will never realize the complete fullness of the power of God's Word in our time here on earth, but we can increase how much we experience it more today than yesterday. Jesus gave us an example of some of the power of the Word in the Gospel of Mark.

Mark 11:23 (ESV) "Truly I say to you, whoever says to this mountain, 'Be taken up and cast into the sea,' and does not doubt in his heart, but believes that what he says is going to happen, it will be granted him."

Jesus was using the illustration of moving a mountain to tell all Christians that if we will speak the Word of God to our problems, they will move into the sea. This almost sounds like something too good to be true. It seems unbelievable that we could speak God's Word to a problem or challenge, some as large as mountains, and they would move out of the way. How can this be? Remember, God's Word created everything.

At its root, everything is built or created from God's Word—even things like viruses, sickness, and diseases. Am I saying God's Word created sickness and disease? No! Satan perverted things and caused them to become tools of death.

It's imperative to understand that Satan does not have any power in him to create anything. He only can pervert, change, or twist. Sickness and disease came from a distortion of molecules to become viruses and bacteria. However, at their root they are still based on the Word of God. That is why these Words of creation, when believed and unleashed by someone in a relationship with Jesus, can change things in their world, body, or life. Since God's Word created everything, it can change everything. It is all-powerful because it is the basis of creation and is limitless in its power. In three of the four Gospels, we see that the Word will never pass away (Matthew 24:35, Mark 13:31, and Luke 21:33).

How can His Words never disappear? They are limitless in their power. There is nothing that exists that can stop or destroy them. The only thing that renders them powerless is when we don't believe them. By powerless I don't mean they aren't still full of power, but rather the potential power inside them is not accessed. In Jesus' time on the earth, the only time He was stopped from doing something for someone is when they didn't believe Him. In Mark, we see what stops God's power in our world today.

Mark 6:1–6 (NLT) Jesus left that part of the country and returned with his disciples to Nazareth, his hometown. The next Sabbath He began teaching in the synagogue, and many who heard Him were amazed. They asked, "Where did He get all this wisdom and the power to perform such miracles?" Then they scoffed, "He's just a carpenter, the son of Mary and the brother of James, Joseph, Judas, and Simon. And His sisters live right here among us." They were deeply offended and refused to believe in Him. Then Jesus told them, "A prophet is honored everywhere except in his own hometown and among his relatives and his own family." ***And because of their unbelief, He couldn't do any miracles*** **among them except to place His hands on a few sick people and heal them. And He was amazed at their unbelief.**

If unbelief stopped Jesus from doing something, it will stop the Word from doing something, even though the Word is unlimited in its power!

You must start with the perfect, all-powerful basis of all creation—God's Word! Why? As you can see, God's Word was the first thing unleashed and is what created everything. This same Word is still here, it still has perfect results, and the Word still cannot be limited except by our faith. So, if God unveiled the Word first, that's why it is put in our tank first.

The Word Must Be Received and Followed as Instruction

The Word of God is not just pretty letters and poetic language written in a giant leather bound book. It isn't just a book of stories and nice thoughts for all of us to aim for. If we want to fill ourselves up the way God intended, the Word must be followed as instructions.

Romans 15:1–4 (NLT) We who are strong must be considerate of those who are sensitive about things like this. We must not just please ourselves. We should help others do what is right and build them up in the Lord. For even Christ didn't live to please himself. As the Scriptures say, "The insults of those who insult you, O God, have fallen on me." Such things were written in the Scriptures long ago *to teach us*. And the Scriptures give us hope and encouragement as we wait patiently for God's promises to be fulfilled

It is plain to see that the Word will give one hope, but when? Millions have lived and read the Word but still had no hope. As I stated earlier, it isn't the religious act of reading scripture that gives us hope. The Word must be read with faith and followed as instruction.

When we follow the instructions found in the Word, that is when the hope God has designed for us begins to bubble up on the inside. The instruction in the Word will teach us how to live, get closer to God, face challenges, treat others, discover our real self, or light our path that the Holy Spirit is leading us down. But if that instruction is never followed, the hope cannot come. The Bible is limitless in its power, but the Word does not function like a magic word. You can't say "abracadabra" and expect it to work.

If someone is putting together a piece of furniture or toy for their child, doesn't it make them feel more confident when they read and follow the directions? Gone are the days at my house when I put something together and have a bag full of parts left over, while the table is leaning heavily to one side. Why? Because I follow directions and I feel way more confident about these projects at my house.

The more we receive the Word as instruction, the more confident we will become in our walk with God. Instruction on *how* to live will make us more confident in the *way* we live. That confidence brings hope and growth in your relationship with God.

Chapter 4

What Are the Benefits to Reading the Bible?

The Word Has the Ultimate Impact on the Believer

In its creative, perfect, and limitless power, there is a measure of that power that has a specific purpose. This specific purpose will bring the greatest impact on the development of you as a believer.

God's Word has the ultimate impact on you as someone who has a relationship with Jesus. Another reason you must read your Bible is because you cannot have strong faith without it and everything in God's kingdom operates on faith.

Romans 10:17 (NLT) ... so then faith comes from hearing and hearing the *Word* of God.

Part of God's Word is specifically designed to build your faith. Why is a whole measure of the Word meant to build your faith? So that you can wield the rest of the Word's power in your life. I like the word "wield" although it is not used regularly anymore. I think of King Arthur wielding "mighty Excalibur" or Thor wielding his hammer, "Mjolnir," and countless other larger-than-life stories where a word like that is used.

The word wield means, "to hold and use." This is what our faith does. It allows us to hold and use the rest of the limitless power found in the Word of God. The only thing that "puts a throttle on" or controls how much of the Word's power operates in our lives is our faith. The only way to get stronger faith is by the input of God's Word. *The limitless immeasurable power in the Word is for us in every area of life today. Every bit of the Word is for us, who are in a relationship with Jesus, to possess, to enjoy, to guide our lives, and to surround ourselves continually with.*

The only problem is we can't begin to contain the power on our own. As fragile human beings, we cannot begin to control or understand the power of the Word of God with human intellect and understanding. We can't earn the Word's rewards by our own good efforts and will power. This is the fallacy of those who try to understand Christianity without a relationship with Jesus. It takes faith for the power of God to operate in the life of the believer.

We lack the power, in and of ourselves, to enjoy or initiate any of the power or blessings of God in each of our lives. If we did have complete faith, we would already have anything and everything we would ever want or need. We would understand the mysteries of God and have an intense relationship with Him like Adam and Eve did. To quote a great mentor of mine, Brian Klemmer, "We would all be skinny, rich, and happy."

As I mentioned earlier, Adam and Eve were *very* close to God in a way nobody else has been. Here is the good news; through our faith, this kind of relationship is possible to have again. This is what a measure of the Word of God does. It builds our faith so that we can enjoy the blessings and power from the Bible in our lives here and now. Then we can apply it as a standard for our lives.

My boys, at the time of this writing, are eight and four years old. They are both old enough to get into the refrigerator and get what they want. Both are big-time cereal eaters. I laugh when I see them get the box of cereal out of the pantry because I remember sitting in front of the television as a kid and eating cereal before school or on a Saturday morning watching *Scooby Doo*.

Preston and Peyton both can carry the box of cereal easily, but both struggle with the gallon of milk. Preston does okay if it's half-full or less but Peyton struggles unless it's almost empty. Both will pull the jug out and drag it across the floor wanting Jodi or me to pour it into their cereal. They are not strong enough to pour the milk themselves. However, the vitamins and nutrients in the milk will make the boys stronger and cause them to keep growing if they will keep drinking it. (After all, "Milk. It does a body good!" Right?) Eventually they will be strong enough to pick up a full gallon and pour it themselves.

This is how the power of the Word of God affects Christians. Our faith may not be strong enough to access all the Word's power or enjoy all the blessings in God's Word. In fact, with the state the world is in, I would say that is obvious. The blessings of God are not evident, to

God's full intention, in our lives yet. However, if the goal is to get there then we must keep filling ourselves with the Word. Our faith will get stronger and stronger until we can have and enjoy every promise and blessing found in it.

This measure of the Word that builds our faith affects every area of our Christian walk. Many famous ministers have spoken about the benefit of faith in prosperity, healing, and deliverance. But there is more to it than that. The Word will build strong faith to receive better understanding of the Word. The Word will build strong faith to grow us closer in our relationship with God. The Word will build strong faith to see every answer that is found in the Word become a reality in our lives. This measure of the power of the Word allows us to wield—to hold and use—the rest of its power.

God's Word Is a Roadmap for Your Life That Will Last Forever

The Bible contains answers and instructions that show you how to interact with people, obtain and manage material possessions, live life to the fullest, and face all challenges. God did not leave you to figure this whole thing out on your own. God laid it out for you in His Word.

The Bible is not a book full of fantastic fairytale-type stories. The Word of God is not just a holy book. The Bible is a personal letter to us who believe. These stories and the power contained in them to change our lives, give us a foundation to build upon, and show us what steps to take in our lives.

2 Timothy 3:16 (NLT) *All Scripture* is inspired by God and *is useful to teach us what is true and to make us realize what is wrong in our lives*. It corrects us when we are wrong and teaches us to do what is

right.

God placed in the Word everything we need to make decisions, build relationships, overcome challenges, and live our lives. There are thorough examples and thoughts God had for how to do just about anything. Just because many of these examples are thousands of years old does not mean they are obsolete. These thoughts and ideas will outlast everything else. The information contained in the Bible is relevant forever, even if society wants to explain it away.

Psalm 100:5 (NKJV) For the Lord is good, his mercy is everlasting; *and his truth endures to all generations.*

Truth does not cease to exist because it is ignored or because humanity cannot stomach it. Truth is not relative to opinion. The Bible is still relevant after all this time. It will be relevant forever and its teachings will always be the moral compass and the answer to life's challenges.

God's Word Is the Same Language He Uses in Leading a Christian

When we grow and mature in our walk with God, there comes a time we begin to be led by the Holy Spirit. Believe it or not, every believer has direct access to the Holy Spirit and can be individually led and directed.

How awesome would it be if you *had* to decide something, to have someone feeding you the answer? Every believer can have that experience. Being led by the Holy Spirit is mentioned again and again in the Scripture. When we come to that place in our walk with God, it is imperative to have a filter in place to filter out our thoughts and desires so we can figure out what God is leading us to do.

Proverbs 20:27 (NKJV) The spirit of a man is the lamp of the Lord, searching all the inner depths of his heart.

Romans 8:14 (NLT) For all who are led by the Spirit of God are children of God.

What does it mean to be led by the Holy Spirit? This is quite an extensive subject but in short, each Christian, after we are born again, are returned to the same state that Adam and Eve were created in; a state where we can have regular communication with God. The biggest difference between Adam and Eve and believers now is once we accept Jesus, we are recreated on the inside and the communication with God is predominately done on a spiritual level.

This spiritual interaction is also how God speaks to each of us. When God speaks back and gives information or instruction to us, *that is being led by the Holy Spirit*. Being led by Him is when we have, for lack of a better term, an "inner feeling" or an "inward knowing" about something in our lives without knowing how we know it. Some call it a hunch, a feeling, or a leading. It is much like the ultimate high speed Wi-Fi connection to the source of all knowledge, love, and wisdom.

However, many people substitute completely hearing from God this way for reading God's Word. When we choose one over the other, it will lead to extremes and problems. Many seem to forget the vocabulary God uses to speak to us is the same vocabulary found in His Word. Before you freak out, when I say vocabulary I don't mean God speaks with a King James accent and says, "thee" and "thou." I mean *the message of His leading will always agree with the message in His Word.*

It will not be different. God's leading will never go against His Word.

If you are being "led" to do something and what you feel led to do does not line up to the Bible, then God is not leading you that way. His Word is the standard by which He leads *all* believers. He will *always* speak the same way He does in Scripture. Therefore, it takes a commitment to read your Bible to be familiar with the way God speaks.

I grew up in Kentucky where there are a lot of country accents. A country accent is not the same as a Southern accent. The first time I met someone from Alabama I instantly knew they were not from Kentucky. As I further expanded my horizons, I began to meet people from the Northeast who don't sound like someone from Kentucky at all. Whenever I meet people from another country, it is obvious they are not from the same place as me. Why is it so obvious? Because it does not sound the same as the spoken words which I'm familiar with.

In the same way, if we want to be familiar with the leading of the Holy Spirit, we must stay in the Word of God. If we stay in the Word and a thought or hunch comes, we can easily identify it as being God or not. Why? Because it will either sound just like His Word or nothing like His Word.

What does God sound like? Audibly, I have no idea. I have a grand image of God's voice being a hybrid of Darth Vader and Barry White, but I can honestly say I don't think I have ever heard His voice. However, I can say I have been led and have had a clear thought drop into my spirit that I could identify as God because it was a very similar thought communicated in scripture.

God's Word Will Shed Light on the Path of Life

Psalm 119:105 (NLT) Your word is a lamp to guide my feet and a light for my path.

At our church, we use the phrase "Journey Together" quite often. In that statement, we are telling everyone that all of us are on a journey which ends in one of two places—Heaven or Hell. On the path believers follow, Christians should be helping each other along the way. That path, even though it is righteous or godly, is still in the middle of a dark world. This darkness is something every Christian is dealing with, although the attacks may be stronger or weaker during different seasons of your life.

Darkness can cause us to be unsure of things in our lives. How do we handle a problem? How do we identify God's desires or our selfish desires? How do we enjoy life? Life is full of questions that have answers covered in darkness. However, this will not always be the case and many of the answers can come unveiled the more familiar we become with the Word.

1 Corinthians 13:12 (NLT) *Now we see things imperfectly*, like puzzling reflections in a mirror, but then we will see everything with perfect clarity. *All that I know now is partial and incomplete*, but then I will know everything completely, just as God now knows me completely.

The Bible calls us as believers "children of light" in a world that is in darkness. The one sure light we have full access to right now, that will cause each of us to see the twists, turns, and potholes on the path of life is God's Word. If God mentions it in His Word, then it is important enough to take note of that topic. Then when something happens in our lives, whether good or bad, we can understand it better the more we grow in our understanding of the Word. Why? God's Word will show us what God thinks about what we are dealing with. Those thoughts come straight from God's heart and when we begin to see what God thinks we can learn how to deal with it.

On TV or in the movies, how do they show someone has finally understood something? A light bulb appears over their head and it's usually partnered with a "ding" noise. That image is communicating the idea of "Aha! I see it," or "Now I get it!" This is what God's Word does for believers; the Word causes life's path to be illuminated! It allows us to grow closer in our relationship with Him and we begin to see what God thinks about what we are experiencing. When life's path is illuminated by God's Word, we can stand and fight, sit back and enjoy, thank God, or blame the devil.

God's Word Will Identify Sin So We Can Walk Away from It

As I said earlier, sin is what separated humanity from God. God knew He was separated from everyone and desired to fix it. Jesus became sin for everyone, but He also defeated all of sin's power over those who would believe in Him. If the power of sin is broken, do believers need to even be concerned with it? The answer is yes, and no. I'll explain.

Yes we do, in the fact we can't just act however we want, do whatever we want, believe whatever we want, and still think everything will be ok because sin's power has been destroyed. The Bible is the standard of identifying sin.

However, we as believers don't have to be so concerned with sin that we live in fear of messing up. Everyone sins every day without realizing it. It is these sins we do not need to be concerned about. That is what the grace of God is for—to help us in the areas we may be completely ignorant about or have not been able to overcome yet, but are still trying. The Word of God is how we are to recognize and walk away from sin.

Psalm 119:11 (NKJV) Your word I have hidden in my heart, that I might not sin against you.

1 John 2:1 (NLT) My dear children, *I am writing this to you so that you will not sin*. But if anyone does sin, we have an advocate who pleads our case before the Father. He is Jesus Christ, the one who is truly righteous.

There are many things the Word teaches and clearly identifies as sin. You may ask, "How can you know what those things are if you aren't reading the Word?" I believe many people's lives stay in a state of upheaval because they don't read the Word so they don't know the truth. There are so many people who do not know what God's Word says. They fail to learn what God has said is a sin, or what things to avoid.

The Word is the filter through which we must examine our actions. God spoke and someone wrote it down and now we, as believers, can know. The Word—when read, learned, and deposited within our hearts—causes our filter of sin to come into agreement with God's filter. At this point, God's way of living begins to make sense to our spirits as believers. John said the Word was written to help us not to sin. The Word then becomes the judge by which we examine our actions.

John 12:48 (NKJV) He who rejects Me, and does not receive My

words, has that which judges him—*the word that I have spoken will judge him in the last day.*

If the Word says not to do something, it's safe to say it shouldn't be done. In no uncertain terms is that negotiable. Some may read that and think, "Well, what do I do now? I see there are things I know are sin but I can't just stop." Does that mean that person is hopeless? On the surface and without knowing how good God is, you might think that. I believe that's why the world is full of disillusioned people who are ready to give up. But God is not ready to cut everyone off and send them to hell at the drop of a hat.

If you begin to believe you are not living up to the standard of the Bible, get in line. No one—including myself, your pastor and the preachers you see on television—is living at that standard completely. Every believer is in the middle of a life-long process to accept and live up to it. But we do have to begin the process of bringing ourselves up to God's standard. The Bible speaks about this extensively.

Romans 6:6 (NLT) We know that our old sinful selves were crucified with Christ so that sin might lose its power in our lives. We are no longer slaves to sin.

Galatians 5:24 (NLT) Those who belong to Christ Jesus have nailed the passions and desires of their sinful nature to his cross and crucified them there.

Ephesians 4:22 (NLT) Throw off your old sinful nature and your former way of life, which is corrupted by lust and deception.

Colossians 3:5 (NLT) So put to death the sinful, earthly things

lurking within you. Have nothing to do with sexual immorality, impurity, lust, and evil desires. Don't be greedy, for a greedy person is an idolater, worshiping the things of this world.

Many ministers have used a plethora of terms to describe this process, but it's called *sacrifice* and the Bible strengthens a believer to do it. Each of these passages reference the actions of a believer. As a believer, we must know that our old sinful nature was crucified with Christ. We must nail the passions and desires of our sinful nature to Jesus' cross. We must throw off our old sinful nature and former way of life and put to death the sinful, earthly things living within us. That means each of us has the largest part to play in our own spiritual development.

Sacrifice is not an easy thing to do. But the great thing about God is He wrote the Word to not only point out what a sin is, but He also placed inside that same Word a power that strengthens every believer to walk away from sin. Never is it ok to violate what Jesus commanded us to do.

John 13:34 (NLT) So now I am giving you a new commandment: Love each other. Just as I have loved you, you should love each other.

You might ask, "What about the Ten Commandments?" Jesus wrapped up all ten of them with this one verse. If you love God or another person as Jesus loved them, you will never break any of the Ten Commandments. If you follow the command of love, you would never worship another God, never use the Lord's name in vain, never not keep the Sabbath as holy, never not honor your parents, never murder, never commit adultery, never steal, never lie about someone else, never plot to take someone else's belongings. If you do something that violates the commandment of love, you can be sure it is a sin. However, when you have the Word in your heart, you will continue to grow and improve your ability to recognize your actions as being sin or not.

There are many scriptures in the Bible that say, "You shall not..." or "The Lord does not allow..." However, these are not all talking about sin per se. Sometimes God was referring to specific things He expected of His people while in battle, settling the Promised Land, or for a specific moment. Some of those things would not be a sin now unless God was dealing with you specifically about them. Keep in mind though that the specific leadings of God telling us to not do something will *always* line up with the teachings of the Bible.

I remember when I was growing up, God was dealing with my pastor about not watching television. He said he believed God wanted him to sacrifice TV for a while. After a time of arguing with God, he finally became so convicted by the Holy Spirit he would say, "For me, watching television is a sin." It was a personal conviction specifically led by the Holy Spirit. Nowhere in the Bible will you find a verse that says watching television is a sin.

However, the Bible does say in James 4:17, *"Remember, it is sin to know what you ought to do and then not do it."* (NLT) Even things never addressed in the Word can be shown to us as sin, but if we don't know the standard of the Word, we will have a harder time identifying those things. When the Word is deposited within us, not only will it direct our paths, but it will also judge our actions and identify things we have no business doing and strengthen us so that we can overcome it.

God's Word Shows Us the Difference Between Our Desires and His

Too often, when someone wants to live for God they will ask this question, "How do I know the difference between what I want and what God wants?" This is the million-dollar question. If we completely figured that out, our lives would be mistake-free and filled with the fullness of God's blessings. Unfortunately, arriving at that kind of complete understanding will never happen to us in this life. However, the Word does cause growth in our spirit which allows us to hear more clearly from God and keep our desires in check. How?

Hebrews 4:12 (NKJV) For the Word of God is living and powerful, and shaper than any two-edged sword, piercing even to the division of soul and spirit, and of joints and marrow, and is a discerner of the thoughts and intents of the heart.

This verse talks about a lot of things being separated or being able to tell the difference between them. First, it speaks of the soul and spirit. Many have been raised to believe those two things are the same. They are not. The spirit is the part that God breathed into our bodies to make it alive—the part that comes from God and talks to God. The soul is the bridge from the spirit to the body. The soul is also called the emotions or mind. It is not the brain.

The brain is the organ where the mind operates, but the brain can be damaged and a person can still have their mind. There have been cases where people have had damage to their brain that limited their communication to the outside world. Through technology these brain damaged individuals could connect with the outside world again. Many have been found to have their mind still intact.

The Word has the power to show us the difference in a thought from our own desires and a thought God is speaking to us through the Holy Spirit. That is why the author of Hebrews used the words "joints and marrow." A joint in the body is on the outside where two bones connect. Marrow is something inside the bone.

The writer also used the phrase "thoughts and intents of the heart." What is the writer of Hebrews trying to say? When we consistently put the Word into our hearts, we will grow to understand the difference between our desires and God's desires. We will begin to look at decisions we are making through the filter of God's Word. When challenges arise, we begin to see them the way they are written about in God's Word and what steps need to be taken to get around them. When that filter of the Word is in place, our desires will cause unrest on the inside of us. This happens because we begin to see how our desires do not always line up with the teachings of God's Word.

Chapter 5

Excuses for Not Reading the Bible

At the time I wrote this book, they were beginning the widening of Interstate-4, which goes right through the heart of Orlando, Florida. In fact, Interstate-4 runs from Daytona Beach all the way to Tampa and that stretch is known as the I-4 corridor. My church is not too far from I-4, and getting there during rush hour is bad enough. However, rush hour during the construction has just been plain impossible. The stoppage starts about 15 miles away from our exit, and it is just awful. If you don't prepare yourself to go around, you will be stuck behind miles of cars with no way to get off the road because of the barrier of traffic.

As I said earlier, youth pastors have been preaching, "Read your Bible and pray," forever. Unfortunately, there have been many barriers people put into place to overlook the importance of filling themselves with God's Word. Of those barriers, I want to talk about three that I see as being consistently present in people's lives, no matter where they are in their walk with God.

#1 Arrogance: "I Already Know That!"

The first one I see often enough is arrogance. The attitude of "already knowing that" or "I have already heard that from someone else." Arrogance is defined as "the quality of having or revealing an exaggerated sense of one's own importance or abilities; conceit, pride, self-importance, egotism." It is arrogant to have an attitude that it is a waste of time to read a book written thousands of years ago and expect that it would have any positive effect on our lives today.

Even more arrogant are Christians who believe the Word is for them, but will overlook or skip over the things they used to believe with a passion early in their Christian walk. These people will "move on to something deeper." They use phrases like "I have moved beyond that idea. That elementary truth in the Word doesn't give me what I need anymore. I need deeper truths."

Both mindsets are arrogant. I even heard recently that someone—good Christian people, in fact—has been telling their children that they don't need to believe the Bible or read some of the Bible because that isn't how God talks anymore. This arrogance of beginning to believe that human thinking can ever explain it all or explain some of it away is sad. God can't and won't do anything for those who are arrogant concerning His Word.

Proverbs 16:18 (NLT) Pride goes before destruction, and haughtiness before a fall.

James 4:6 (NLT) And He gives grace generously. As the Scriptures say, "God opposes the proud but gives grace to the humble."

Why would God not do something for someone in pride? Don't they need Him as well? Absolutely they do, and probably more so than ever. However, *faith cannot live, grow, or work, in the heart of an arrogant person because their belief is planted firmly in themselves.* If someone "already knows that," they will not look to see what the Word is saying to them today. God is not interested in what someone knows. If they know it, then they don't need faith or to believe for it.

Faith is defined as "a firm persuasion, a conviction based on hearing." Faith is having a belief based on hearing, or having it communicated to us in some fashion. Anything else is not faith or believing, but instead it is knowing. Knowing and believing are two different things. What someone knows doesn't interest God. Believing in Him and believing on Him does. A person cannot simply *know* what God's Word says and please God. They must believe what God's Word says to please God because it is faith alone that pleases Him.

Hebrews 11:6 (NKJV) But without faith it is *impossible* to please Him, for he who comes to God must believe that He is, and that He is a rewarder of those who diligently seek Him.

This doesn't mean knowledge is bad, but when we base our intimacy in the Word of God upon what we already know, we are building our walk with God on faith in ourselves. Faith in what we already know and not allowing God to reveal Himself fresh and new to us through His Word is not pleasing to Him.

What we understood today while reading the Word isn't what we might understand tomorrow. Because God's Word is alive, we must keep our faith based on new revelation of it, because what is revealed increases over time. A deeper understanding of the Word is what we must strive to achieve, and that can't be achieved based on what we already know. A *complete* understanding will never be achieved in this life. The truth is being revealed more fully each time the Word is read. That is an act of faith, not an act of knowledge.

What we have read and comprehended from the Word today is not the full understanding of the living Scripture. The Word was alive before anyone was born and will be alive after all of creation is gone. Whatever we can comprehend when we read it is not all there is to it. No one will ever exhaust the full content of what God meant in His Word.

When it comes to reading the Bible, we must become humble. What we think we know is a fraction of what is in the Word. A simple prayer asking God to show you more of Himself and the Word's meaning when you read it, will be answered by God every single time. The Scripture says God gives more grace to the humble (James 4:6). He gives more grace to those who keep going back again and again seeking to get filled with the wisdom found in His Word. That grace will shed new light and truth. Then we will learn, grow, and be filled with faith!

#2 Ignorance: "It's Too Hard to Understand!"

In the two plus decades I spent in full-time youth ministry I heard time and time again, "Brent, I want to read the Bible, but I just don't understand it." As a pastor, I am shocked at how many adults say the same thing: "I just don't get it," or "It's really hard to understand." If you have a hard time understanding the Bible, you would probably admit it is very tempting to stop reading it. I can't stress this enough—*don't stop reading it!*

There are many translations of the Bible, from beautiful poetic type language, to common everyday speech, to expanded and amplified language. Find a translation that works for you. I am not someone who bashes on the King James Version as being archaic or the modern translations for watering it down. I have seen people dramatically transformed from both. Whatever translation God uses to bring His Word alive to you is the right translation for you. I have changed translations more than once in my life for my daily reading.

I believe a translation issue is only part of the problem. It goes much deeper than "thee" and "thou." People who stop reading the Bible because they don't understand it will *neve*r come to a place where they *will* understand the Bible. How will you ever understand the Word if you never read it? True understanding comes from within. You can't have it within unless you place it there.

Psalm 119:130 (NKJV) The entrance of your word brings light.

If you don't put the Word inside you, the light can't come. Therefore, you will stay empty and in the dark if you won't read it. If you stop reading it because you don't understand it, you will never be able to believe what belongs to you, what benefits Jesus purchased with His death on the cross, or what rights as a believer you have. You can't speak to a mountain-sized problem unless you know what to say to the mountain. You can't accept healing unless you understand what God's will is concerning healing. You can't have your needs met unless you believe God will supply those needs. You can't have joy in the face of despair unless you believe joy is for you. The only way to know what God wants in *every* area of life is by finding out what God's Word says. Hopefully that helps you see the absolute importance of reading the Word.

The Word of God can't fill you by osmosis. It can't fill you just from being around it. If you depend solely on what you hear preached at church, you will never have strong faith. The only way you will ever understand the Bible is through the process of filling yourself with the Word and overcoming the ignorance of not understanding it.

#3 Disrespect: "I Need Some *Real* Help!"

Since I have been in ministry, I've had people say to me time and time again, "That's good, but can you give me some *real* help?" People say this as if Scripture isn't strong enough to work today. I was speaking to a man who attends my church who was upset about the recent loss of a friend of his who had died from an unusual flesh-eating virus. In his grief, I asked him if his friend knew Christ. He answered that he did and I answered back, "Then you must be comforted by the fact that your friend is not in your past or present but is in your future. Your friend is far better off right now because Paul said that 'To die is gain.'" (Philippians 1:21). He answered, "That will not help his little girl. She is still going to be so upset by this."

First, let me say when grief is at work, it seems like very little will help you feel better or there is very little anyone can say to comfort you no matter where it comes from. However, I do not know how but it seems the Word works in this arena of comforting the loss of someone so much better than you might think.

I asked him this question, "Who are we to say the Word of God won't comfort anyone?" I began to think about how much we limit the Word by downplaying it, when those same words are what created everything and set the world in motion.

Let me say bluntly, *it is disrespectful to consider the Word boring, irrelevant, or having no place in the world in which we live today*. You can't ask for better advice or better help.

I will admit that reading the Bible has not always been the most appealing thing to my flesh, and, therefore, it sometimes can seem boring. Secular and carnal (driven purely by how we feel now) people don't understand the spiritual side of the Bible or the spiritual side of man. Man is a spirit who has been placed in a body by God and given a mind. How can we look at a spiritual writing, given to us from the Father of spirits, and fully comprehend it with a natural mind? To say it is irrelevant is showing a carnal nature.

Our flesh doesn't like to read the Bible because it wants to do whatever it wants to do, whenever it wants to do it. This is where discipline enters the picture. If we are going to live a life of being filled, we can't disrespect the Bible by viewing it as archaic and irrelevant to our world today. Every verse, sentence, and teaching is for humanity *today*. There isn't a part of the Bible that doesn't apply to life.

No part of the Bible needs an apology. Every part of the Word should be offered to help people. The whole council of the Word should be presented and we should read the whole thing. Why would we not offer the very answer for which the world is desperate and needs the most? Every Word in the Bible is more relevant than the most creative sermon or non-abrasive church service anyone could ever hear or attend. I am not saying the church should preach beyond the basics to new believers, but we shouldn't leave them with just the basics for years or decades.

The Bible speaks to the newest Christian, as well as to the most advanced Saint. To apologize for part of the perfect word of God, or to never present it because it may offend, is disrespectful to the Word, God, and the receiver. The Church isn't doing anyone any favors by not encouraging people to read the whole thing and attempt to apply all the Bible to their lives.

The Bible and its message are offensive to our flesh because Christians are in the process of changing to become more like Jesus. Considering the perfection of God's Word, flaws in our human character are noticed. Those areas in our lives that need to change are obviously offended by it. Our flesh should always be offended by the Word. What is offensive to our flesh, however, is uplifting and encouraging to the real person God created and placed in this flesh—our spirit.

Does that mean the Word is irrelevant because it is offensive to our flesh? No! In fact, that's even more reason to embrace its relevancy in life! We need to change to live life more and more closely to the guidance of God's Word. From the beginning of time, people have looked to the comfort of their flesh to judge whether something is acceptable. This is the wrong filter to apply. Listening to the flesh has led people to being overweight, addicted to vices, overly sensitive, easily offended, absent-minded, and spoiled. Just because the flesh doesn't like something doesn't mean that thing shouldn't be included in life.

When people who call the Bible irrelevant have a hard challenge come their way, they will covet the prayers of people who build their lives around the Bible. When we are full of the Word and pressure comes from challenges, that pressure will cause the Word to come out of our mouths, enter our thoughts, and sway the situation.

My questions for you are:

- What usually comes out of you when a bad situation hits?
- Have you been disrespectful to the Word as being irrelevant?
- When the pressures of life come are you getting angry, cussing, producing fear, and words filled with doubt?
- Or when pressure arises, are you confidently saying the perfect, all-powerful, creative Word of God which has built your faith?
- When pressure arises, are you filled with the Word of God enough that your response to the pressure is based on that Word?

Chapter 6

How to Read the Word

As we approach the first one-quarter filling mark, I want to give some practical advice on reading the Word so that you can achieve the full Christian life the way God intends.

The first thing I would recommend is read an abbreviated version of our redemption. Start in the story of creation! You must understand the story in Genesis—the first three chapters in particular—because that is where the mess mankind is in came from. This sets up the most important part of creation; once sin happened, mankind needed a savior.

When you understand that what happened in Genesis was the framing of the world and man placing it into the bondage of sin, then you should switch to the Gospels—Matthew, Mark, Luke, and John. I personally recommend the Gospel of John after reading Genesis 1 through 3, then follow that with the other three Gospels.

You might ask, “Why are there four versions of the story?” Many have said the Gospels are like four individuals witnessing an event and then retelling the same story from their point of view. Matthew might have noticed something Mark didn’t and so forth. Four gospels give a well-rounded view of the life, death, and resurrection of the Savior we all need. It is necessary to understand the first three chapters of Genesis and the four Gospels of Matthew, Mark, Luke, and John.

After that is clear, I recommend getting a better understanding of what this new relationship with Him does for you. That revelation can be found mostly in the writings of Paul known in a little anagram called, “God’s Electric Power Company!” Take the first letter of each word and you get the same first letter in four writings of Paul that are in the middle of the New Testament: Galatians, Ephesians, Philippians, and Colossians. These four books contain a major revelation that is lacking in the Church today. It is called the “in Christ” revelation. In these four writings, Paul unveils who Christians are, what Christians have, and what Christians should be able to do because they belong “in Christ.”

Start with these recommendations and keep reading them over and over for the first three months.

After you grab the basics and the “in Christ” revelation, my advice is to move on to Acts to see what else is available to you after you believe in Jesus. After that, read the rest of the New Testament, and then the Old Testament. After Genesis, it is the long story of God fulfilling His promise of redemption to all of mankind and all the details that went into making that promise a reality.

Don't Try to Read the Whole Thing at Once

When I first started living for God again, I remember being overwhelmed with how much of the Bible I should be reading because I knew I couldn't read a lot without my mind wandering. I eventually decided that when my mind started to wander, I would hold it there for a few minutes, to discipline myself, but at the same time I knew I was nearing the end of that day's read. You do not have to read the whole Bible today! Read what you can without your mind wandering from a translation you enjoy. The King James is not more "holy" than modern translations. You may like one of them better and that is ok. Train your mind to stay focused, but understand the process is going to take time. Today, my *personal* reading and study lasts about 30 minutes. This does not include sermons, study and preparation. This is just God and me filling my tank and building my relationship. You can do it too, even if you're starting at 5 minutes and half of a chapter. Stay with it; you will grow!

Get on a Plan

After you grasp the basics, my advice is to start putting the Word into your heart on a wholesale basis. Read it as much as you can. Download a Bible app and have it read the Word to you. A good one is the You Version app, available in the App Store and Google Play Store. Get a "one-year" Bible and read the whole thing in 365 days. The more you put the word in, the more it begins to produce positive, God-centered change and fill you with the life God intended you to have.

Half a Tank: Time Spent with God

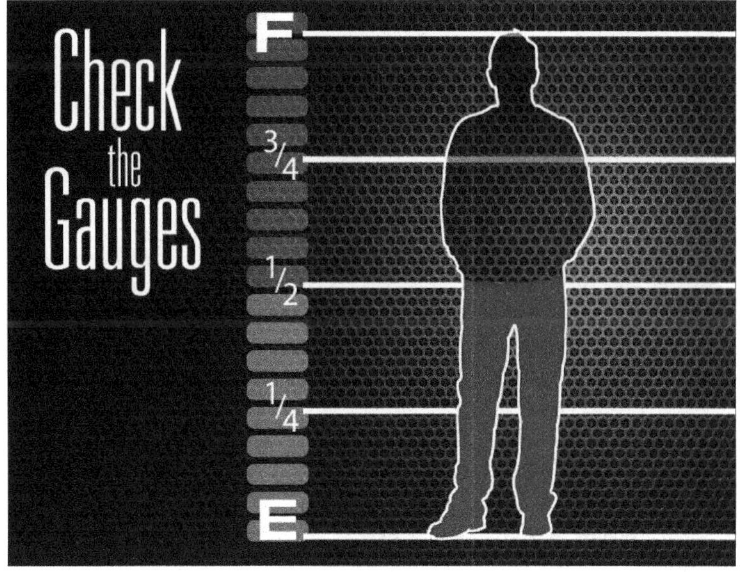

Chapter 7

Time with God Will Change You

To get yourself to half a tank on your way to becoming filled the way God intended, you must spend time with God in prayer and in worship. When you do, not only does it further your relationship with Him, but it also causes you to change. It is impossible to be in the presence of God without it affecting you greatly. Throughout the Bible we see a lot of examples of people being changed when they were in the presence of God.

> Adam and Eve didn't realize they were naked. (Genesis 2:25)
> Enoch and Elijah both left the earth without dying. (Genesis 5:24, 2 Kings 2:11)
> Moses face literally glowed. (Exodus 34:29–35)

The priests couldn't stand up to minister. (2 Chronicles 5:14, 2 Chronicles 7:2, 1 Kings 8:11)
David's heart became like God's. (Acts 13:22)
Mary became pregnant. (Luke 1:26–38)
The Roman soldiers were knocked down. (John 18:6)
Jesus' body became unrecognizable. (Luke 24:16)
The 12 disciples became batteries of God's power to the point where they performed many miracles. (Acts 5:12)
Peter's shadow healed people. (Acts 5:15)
One hundred twenty believers in the upper room spoke in tongues and nearly a whole international city, full of international guests, heard them speaking about the goodness of God in their own language, dialogue, and accent. (Acts 2)
Paul was knocked off his horse, blinded, and changed from being the original terrorist against Christians to the Church's greatest Apostle. (Acts 9, Acts 19:11)

These incredible changes came from spending time in the presence of God. A lot of people regulate time with God to asking for help or for something. Sure, that's part of it, but that's not all there is to it. Many people think reading the Word is all there is too. They don't expect God to spend time with them.

We've discussed the importance of the Word and how everything else should be filtered through it. However, when we receive a word from God in our heart or see something in the Word we never saw before, that is God strengthening our faith in an area where our faith is lacking. Our faith needs to be strengthened every day, which is why we should start in the Word. However, spending time with God is different.

When we spend time with God, we are spending time in the presence of the One where all the power comes from—the One who spoke out the words that fill up the Bible, the One who created everything, who heals the sick, who meets all needs, who reveals things that are hidden, who gives joy to the depressed, fixes the broken, helps the helpless, promotes the forgotten, removes the stress, solves the problem, moves the mountains, and so much more.

We as human beings have been created to absorb and contain whatever environment we are in. When we are in a hot room, we get hot and will remain hot until the environment changes. How many times during the summer have you gone to your car and it was just as hot inside the car as it was outside? You didn't get any relief from the heat inside the car until you changed the environment. You couldn't get the air conditioning on or those windows down fast enough.

What are you doing in that instance? You are trying to *change the environment* because you absorbed and contained the environment you are in.

These are physical changes, but it's the same emotionally. When we are around an emotional situation, we will absorb the same emotions until the environment changes.

I'm sure most people have experienced this at funerals, weddings, birthday parties, and so on. I've felt fine before walking in the door at a funeral, but before long I'm crying or have become very somber at a funeral for someone I barely knew. Likewise, I've become happy at a birthday party for a small child who is friends with one of my sons.

God created us to be containers. We take on the physical and emotional characteristics of the environment we are in. Therefore, it is so important for us to put ourselves in an environment with God. We can't put ourselves into His presence without absorbing His power, character, and goodness. That would be like placing a bucket in a pool and not expecting it to fill up with water.

We can't be in the God's presence and not become more like Him. We were created by Him to hold His presence. If we are going to be filled the way He created us to be, we must fill ourselves with His presence. From what you've already read, you know spending time in the Word is the first way to be fill with God. Now I'd like to share two others with you—prayer and worship.

Chapter 8

Communicating with God

As a child of the 70's, teenager of the 80's, and young adult of the 90's, I will admit I grew up listening to secular radio. I understand if you want to put this book down now because it's hard to receive from someone who used to be such a dirty, rotten sinner. (Ha-ha!) I used to justify it when any song mentioned praying or God, even the ones that were not referring to God the way we do.

I remember in 1986 when Bon Jovi's *Slippery When Wet* album came out and the song "Livin' on a Prayer" was number one on our local radio station's "Top Ten at 10" for several nights in a row. That was my excuse to embrace Bon Jovi. My parents hadn't allowed me to go see them in concert the first time they were at the Huntington Civic Center. Finally, a song that would justify it!

I can still hear John Bon Jovi belting it out, "OOOOOOOOOOOOOHH, we're halfway there. OOOOOOHHH-OOOOOOHHH, livin' on a prayer!" (*See what I did there? John singing, "We're halfway there," we're talking about prayer, and it just so happens to be the halfway mark on our tank.)*

There are so many ideas of prayer that aren't right or beneficial to anyone. Prayer is often seen as asking God to help when things aren't going well. It has been portrayed as someone lighting a candle in a chapel or kneeling and looking up with a questionable look on their face. It usually starts with, "God, if You're really there..." or "I'm not really the person who ever does this..."

If you're going to get to the halfway mark, you must understand that prayer is so much more than begging a God you don't know very well for help that He may or may not send.

Praise and worship is also something people have a stereotypical view of. Worship has been painted as the singing part of a church service. You might hear people say, "I love praise and worship at my church." (You might have even said it yourself.) Sometimes it's almost as though that is the only time praise and worship is happening.

But praise and worship is not just singing songs in church before the preaching. Praise and worship is our way as believers to communicate to God the sincere love, appreciation, and acknowledgement of His awesomeness.

The Greek word for praise means to brag on God. You might ask, "Why does God need anyone to brag on Him?" He doesn't. Believe it or not, bragging on God benefits us. Praise verbalizes what we believe about God in our hearts, regardless of what is happening around or to us. Amid everything happening to us, we are still communicating how awesome God is. This verbalizing builds our faith.

Romans 10:17 (NLT) So faith comes from hearing, that is, hearing the Good News about Christ.

When we open our mouth and brag on Him, we are building our faith and the faith of others around us that can hear us. Why is that so important? Because it is in this "atmosphere of faith" that the presence of God shows up.

Psalm 100:4 (NLT) Enter his gates with thanksgiving; go into his courts with praise. Give thanks to him and praise his name.

Praising God brings us into the same shared space with God. That's why we need someone bragging on God, so our faith can be strengthened.

What do we do when we share space with God? We worship Him! Worship literally means to honor, respect, and show true and sincere affection to Him. There are two ways this can happen. We are going to talk about both, but the second one will come later in the book.

The first way though is to show respect and submission by bowing your head, closing your eyes, and/or kneeling. It is our response with everything we are—mind, emotions, will, and body—to everything God is, says, and does.

The example I'm about to give is unusual, but hear me out. Imagine for a second that you're sitting on the sofa and the family dog walks over and begins to stick its nose under your hand just to get interaction with it. That dog will squirm, move, and sometimes lick your hand just to receive a pat, a rubbing of the tummy, or a scratch between the ears because they love you so much.

In a way, that is what worship is. You're willing to do whatever is necessary to show God how much you love Him, like a dog licking his master's hand. I highly doubt God is going to ask any of us to lick his hand, but worship is our willingness to revere Him by bowing our heads, kneeling at our seats, and pouring out our heart's love toward Him.

All three of these things are ways we communicate with God and God communicates with us individually. Spending time with Him is a spiritual act that has spiritual results. We can't spend time with anyone on a one-on-one basis without learning a great deal about them.

We also learn about ourselves. Those of you who have been married can answer this question: Do you remember the first time your spouse finished your sentence? It revealed a closeness in your relationship that came from spending so much time together.

Because spending time with God is a *spiritual* act, it cannot be fully comprehended with the *natural* mind. Many people think spending time with God is just asking for help or singing songs of worship in church. But it is so much more than that.

When someone simplifies spending time with God to things they can understand with their natural mind, they reduce prayer, praise, and worship's power and purpose. But time with God reveals who He *is* and who He *wants to be* to each person.

John 4:24 For God is Spirit, so those who worship Him must worship

in spirit and in truth – (NLT)

Many people make the mistake of employing natural methods to achieve spiritual results. Getting to know God has nothing to do with being good enough, giving enough, going to church enough, stopping bad habits, or any other action. None of these things are going to cause you to know the person of God. These things are the *results* of knowing God, not *qualifications* that allow you to know Him. To think otherwise is backwards.

No matter how "good" you are, you can never be good enough, naturally speaking, to bring about spiritual results. Spiritual results work in the opposite way. God, being a spirit, is looking to change our natural being. We must learn that real change, spiritually speaking, comes first. Therefore, to get to know the person of God, we must invest time with Him personally. The more time we spend with Him, the more our spirits will influence our natural being.

Romans 8:11 (NLT) The Spirit of God, who raised Jesus from the dead, lives in you. And just as God raised Christ Jesus from the dead, he will give life to your mortal bodies by this same Spirit living within you.

The question that comes to mind here is, "What effect does spending time with God really have on us?" To answer that question, we must go back and lean on the ideas presented earlier in this book—every answer concerning anything about God must have its basis in Scripture first.

Spending Time with God Reveals His Thoughts About Us to Us

1 Corinthians 14:2 (NIV) For anyone who speaks in a tongue does not speak to people but to God. Indeed, no one understands them; *they utter mysteries by the Spirit.*

1 Corinthians 14:14–15 (NIV) For if I pray in a tongue, my spirit prays, but my understanding is unfruitful. So what shall I do? I will pray with my spirit, but I will also pray with my understanding; I will sing with my spirit, but I will also sing with my understanding.

1 Corinthians 2:6–9 (NIV) We do, however, speak a message of wisdom among the mature, but not the wisdom of this age or of the rulers of this age, who are coming to nothing. No, we declare God's wisdom, *a mystery* that has been hidden and that God destined for our glory before time began. None of the rulers of this age understood it, for if they had, they would not have crucified the Lord of glory. However, as it is written: "What no eye has seen, what no ear has heard, and what no human mind has conceived the things God has prepared for those who love him."

Spending time with God in prayer reveals mysteries to us that have been previously concealed in the mind of God. There are some things God hasn't spoken or revealed yet. I'm sure people have given much thought about what those are. If everyone in the world was given a microphone and asked, "What are the deep secrets of God?" there would probably be as many different answers as there are people. The answers would be as diverse as things concerning the cosmos and how it operates, what Heaven is like, the inner workings of His kingdom, the future of the Church, the moving of the Spirit, and who killed JFK? These things are all valid ideas of what God is thinking (except for maybe JFK).

For your sake, as a new or developing Christian, I want to propose something a little bit differently. What if I said to you that anything and everything found in creation has already been released from God's mouth, therefore He isn't actively thinking about it. That means the world we live in and all of creation isn't in His mind anymore. Those things are already existing. They are here and now.

The mysteries of the cosmos aren't a mystery to Him because He created them and put them in place. We are still discovering what is there, but to God they are no more a mystery than 2 + 2 is to us. I'm sure many people believe God is thinking about the future of creation, the weather patterns, and what's going to happen on the earth.

But what about this concept? Time is a created force and God operates outside of it. The generalized future of the world isn't a mystery because He created all of it already and it is happening all at once. I have heard the term, "He holds the future." The fact that He is holding it and it is happening all at once is why He can lead people to prepare for the future. He's seeing tomorrow and how it is supposed to happen right now.

Maybe the mysteries of the Bible are what He is thinking about. Nope, that's not it either. He has already spoken it out, and it is not a secret any more. The world may not understand it all, and humanity is still trying to catch up to what it all means, but none of these things are the big mysteries or secrets of God. (It is important to mention here that just because these things are not deep in the mind of God anymore, does not mean that they do not still contain as much power as they ever did.)

So, if prayer is supposed to expose the things on God's mind to us, what in the world are they? I believe we find them in a very popular verse in the Old Testament.

Jeremiah 29:11 (NKJV) For I know the *thoughts* that I think *toward you*, says the Lord, *thoughts of peace and not of evil*, to *give you a future and a hope.*

Who knows God's thoughts? He does! Nobody else knows them, but Him. This is the part that is incredible. The thoughts inside God's mind are all about His children and the plans that He has for everyone! *That means you!*

Prayer unveils mysteries that are deep in the mind of God! Every person and *their* future are what God is thinking about. What He has in store for you, His leading for you, *your* future and hope is what God is thinking about all the time! Therefore, spending time with Him is so important. You are getting to know the One who is thinking and planning a great future *for you.* Time with God starts to reveal those plans.

1 Corinthians 2:10–12 (NLT) But it was to us that God revealed these things by his Spirit. For his Spirit searches out everything and *shows us God's deep secrets.* No one can know a person's thoughts except that person's own spirit, and *no one can know God's thoughts except God's own Spirit. And we have received God's Spirit* (not the world's spirit), ***so we can know the wonderful things God has freely given us.***

Time with God unveils more about what He wants to do in, with, and for *you.* It reveals more than a guidance counselor, aptitude test, prophetic word, or advice from someone could ever reveal.

There is nothing wrong with any of those things, but they should only confirm what God is showing us already in our hearts. Those test results, guidance sessions, and words of advice are wonderful. However, those words are just a glimpse—a movie trailer so to speak. They are a preview of what is potentially going to happen.

Your prayer life is the only thing that can show you the entire movie. If you will spend time with God, you can discover what an *epic* motion picture the plan of God and His thoughts are towards you. The movies *The Ten Commandments*, *Gone with the Wind*, and *Ben Hur* have nothing on the plan God is thinking toward you.

God is still thinking about what He wants you to do with your life, what He wants to do in your life, how He wants to bless your life, and what you can achieve in this life!

The last one is the one not set in stone because God gave us a choice—to choose where we are going and what we are going to do with our lives. Our choices can change the outcome we experience. Not only that, the thoughts God has toward us can be discovered and revealed. Once God's thoughts about you start being revealed to you, then you must decide what to do with those thoughts. Sometimes He may lead you to go back and repent, change directions, correct the way you have been doing something, or something completely different. Your actions after will determine how much of what God was thinking about you will continue to show up in your life.

But this is not the only reason to spend time with God in prayer. We are obviously called to pray for others and this world we live in. However, if we are going to fill ourselves the way God intended, a large portion of our prayer life is developing a personal relationship with God.

Time spent with God is what unveils the mystery of His thoughts toward each of us—great, incredible, and amazing things. When the Word is read, it is a letter from Him that establishes the framework and spiritual laws for God's power to operate. *We can spend time with the One who wrote that letter.* We can have a conversation with Him and learn how those laws and that framework will keep us in line with our specific leadings.

Do you remember when text messaging came out? Wasn't it easier to just pick up the phone and call someone? Text messaging is great at communicating simple messages that do not need a lot of explaining. However, there are still plenty of times where it is easier to pick up the phone and have a thorough conversation. In the same way, there is a lot of important foundational information you can only get from reading the Word of God. But at the same time, the only way to get specific information about your life is through prayer and time spent with God. By spending time with Him, you begin to think more like Him and understand what He's thinking about your life!

Throughout my life, I have had many experiences in which I can remember hitting rough patches on the road of life, stressful times of work, shortages of money, physical illness or injuries, and times where I just wanted to throw in the towel and quit. It's during these rough times I spend even more time with God than I normally do. In the first three weeks of every new year, I do a 21-day fast and it's honestly one of the most rewarding things I do. It is a wonderful time to refocus and seek God in a more intense way. I spend time in the Word, in prayer in my closet, and in a devotional.

One year during this fast, I knew something was happening because every week there was a larger challenge than the week before. This culminated with the final week of my fast. The largest donor at the church I pastor told me he was leaving. This meant that one-third of the church income would no longer be available. It was hard to accept. It was over a doctrinal difference. To be fair, he told me he enjoyed our church but just couldn't get comfortable with us being Spirit-filled.

My world was rocked, but I simply walked back into the closet and began to pray and spend some time with God. I found myself repenting and saying, "God if I have done something to run them off, I'm so sorry." I found myself not wanting to be the spoiled kid who breaks his toys and then demands a new one. I didn't want to be the pastor who runs his people off, and then turns around and says, "Well if they can't get hooked up with what the Holy Spirit is doing, it's their loss."

Unlike the situation I shared with you earlier, in this instance I didn't have any kind of pre-warning in my spirit that something rough was coming. I did what I normally do and dropped to my knees and started praying. While I was praying, I felt led to stop. I was so shocked, I didn't know what to do. I simply obeyed and stopped praying about the situation. I just began to spend time with God to experience more of who He is. I was tempted to make a change in that doctrine that the person had a problem with and back away from it, but I knew that wasn't right. I just kept spending time worshipping God and allowing His presence to be the calm in my storm.

I addressed the church the following Sunday. I told them that we believed in being Spirit-filled and Spirit-led, and that was who we were. We weren't going to change. I just continued to worship God whenever I thought about the situation, and I would thank Him for taking care of us.

That same week, I went to see my pastor who was holding a meeting in St. Augustine, Florida. He spoke an encouraging word that was exactly what I needed to hear. He spoke on Mark 11:23–24, which tells us to speak to our mountain. He emphasized the importance of not becoming separated from what you say, but to keep saying it and it would cause you to have what you say.

Jodi and I began to speak to a mountain of "*lack*" because of the finances that walked out the door of our church. We kept speaking and kept speaking. A few weeks later a pastor friend of mine from the southern part of the United States sent me a text. I want to share with you the exact message. This is what spending time with God does for you in the hard times! He shows who He is and what He thinks about you.

"Hey brother. For quite some time, I've had it on my heart to sow into your church. The Holy Spirit has been leading me to do it, so I'm going to give you two options. I feel led to sow $50,000 into your ministry. I can send you one lump sum or $5000 a month, starting in March until the end of the year."

Now that was enough to make me shout hallelujah from the mountaintops. Too bad there aren't any mountains in Florida. But God is even better than that. This pastor went on to say, "I have it in my heart big to tell you that God is proud of you and that you are headed in the right direction! Don't stop! You are a blessing!" That was such a confirmation to me. I felt such a relief that God was going to take care of us. I was so happy and overwhelmed with emotion that I had to put both hands on my knees and catch my breath like I had just ran a few miles.

God had answered big time.

One month later I had a church member walk up to me unexpectedly and ask, “Has God been dealing with you concerning anything big?” I answered him, “Always! But specifically, what are you talking about?” He went on to tell me how God had spoken to him through something I said at the close of the worship part of our service.

While we were singing, I had felt led to say, “Someone is up for a blessing and it’s just a little further out there than you think. It’s not because it’s being withheld from you, it’s just bigger than you think it is. When you finally get to it, it will be much bigger than you ever thought.”

This gentleman told me he knew I was talking to him and he decided to start spending more time with God in the meantime. When it finally came to pass, his blessing was way bigger than even he thought and he was so happy. He said to me, “The first thing I want to do is pay my tithes on this big blessing, Pastor!” He then handed me a check for $80,000. Again, I was overwhelmed with emotion and literally blown away by God answering in such a strong way.

In 30 days, God supernaturally replaced every cent and then some of the supply that had walked out the door. I don’t claim to understand all that God is, or know all that He knows, but I am convinced that the relationship I have with Him is revealed more to me through prayer and time spent with Him. When He answers, I see a little more what He’s thinking, and I see what His plans are for me!

What an honor to know that God is thinking about our futures! That, accompanied with everything that is happening in the world today, with everyone else that is on planet earth, and with every trial and temptation that comes, God is still thinking about each of us individually!

When the bill pops up, He already thought about it. When we are confused about what we're supposed to do next, He has already thought of that. When we aren't feeling well, He's already thought of it. When we are down in the dumps and facing depression, He's already thought about that too. He's thinking about our hope and future and how to get it into our hands. We are what God has on His mind! God has us on the brain, and He already knows where and what the answers are for our lives!

Spending Time with God is the Relationship-Builder

It is impossible to know someone unless you spend time with them. The more time you spend with a person, you know when something is wrong, or when everything is right, maybe when something is about to change, or when things need improvement.

Imagine a couple when they are first dating. Everything is roses. They are completely showcasing the best version of themselves while on a date. However, there is a side to them that only comes out when they go home and the other person is not around. The guy doesn't know if or when the girl is thinking about him and so he just imagines she is thinking about him all the time, and vice versa.

When they get married and live in the same house, things get revealed. Sometimes it's shocking! He realizes she isn't always thinking about him and he was not the sole focus of her thoughts. Imagine when he is in her presence, and realizes she isn't focused completely on him. At first, he might feel panicked and ask himself, "How could she not be thinking about me all the time?"

The point here is the longer a person is in a relationship with someone, they realize those moments aren't a big deal. Why? Because those people know each other because they have spent so much time together.

This is how things are with God. The more time you spend with Him and become familiar with Him, you can begin to know what He thinks and wants, and what you are supposed to do for Him. This is what praying and spending time with Him does for all of us!

There are still so many things God thinks about that He hasn't told anyone else, but He wants so much to share those things with each of us! When we spend time with Him and a hard time hits, a difficult challenge arises, or a dry season comes, it's no big deal because we know the person of God and who He is. Our relationship has been framed with the Word and built through time spent with Him.

Shared Space with God Confirms Your Relationship

Hebrews 4:14–16 (NLT) So then, since we have a great High Priest who has entered heaven, Jesus the Son of God, let us hold firmly to what we believe. This High Priest of ours understands our weaknesses, for he faced all the same testings we do, yet he did not sin. So let us come boldly to the throne of our gracious God. There we will receive his mercy, and we will find grace to help us when we need it most.

If you have a relationship with Jesus and accept what He did, then you have the right to talk to Him. Prayer is a privilege every believer has—to have a relationship with God and communicate with Him anytime. Somehow people have come to believe that anyone can cry out to God whenever, however, and wherever they are in life. Truthfully, there is nothing in the Bible that says they can't.

However, not just anyone can call on God *with confidence and expect an answer* like those who are in a relationship with Him. Spending time with God is a confirmation of our relationship with Him because we can call on Him and expect a response. We started our relationship with God with a prayer and that's how it flourishes and grows. Praying and spending time with Him are essential to a life filled with His goodness!

If someone is not in a relationship with God, there is only one prayer they can pray and expect a response. If He does answer a prayer for a person that isn't a believer, it's because He is good and merciful. The only prayer He is required to answer from those who aren't in a relationship with Him is found in Romans. Romans 10:13 says, *"Everyone who calls on the name of the Lord will be saved."* (NLT)

They can begin the process of praying and finding out what God thinks about them by accepting what Jesus did in their life. Then, the wealth of what God thinks about them can begin to be revealed. Once they have a relationship with Jesus from prayer, then each prayer they pray and the time they spend with Him will confirm their relationship.

Chapter 9

How Do I Pray?

I remember growing up in church and kneeling on Sunday nights around the altar in corporate church prayer. There was a gentleman named Joe Paul Gibson who was one of the sweetest men you could have ever known. However, this man could pray loud and filled with Scripture. I remember listening to him praying more than praying myself.

In those moments, I thought, *"How in the world does someone get to pray like that?"* It was that kind of praying that caused me to think God could only hear beautiful, loud prayers that made you cry. Apparently, it also didn't hurt to have a white handkerchief to wipe the spit, sweat, and tears off your face while having such passionate interaction with the Creator of the universe. That's where I was wrong.

Although there is absolutely nothing wrong with the way someone else prays, you can't build your prayer life by imitating someone else. Prayer is a deeply personal expression to God and will only develop from being yourself.

The first step to developing your prayer life is to stop comparing your prayers to the way someone else does it. I loved Joe Paul and still have a great relationship with his kids today, but I can't pray like Him. However, I am glad to know that *God can and does still hear me*! What I'm about to say might sound cliché, but it's so true: you must talk to God just like you would talk to anyone else.

Think about it like this: God created you and knows how you talk, how you respond to things in life, and how you are when nobody is looking, doesn't He? Why not just be who you are with God? Many believe God only listens to pretty, religious prayers using a lot of words that sound like they came from the Bible and are dripping with a King James accent. Some people will add "Dear Father," "Mighty God," or things of that nature after each sentence, because they've heard others do it. They think that's what they're supposed to do. No matter where you are in your Christian walk, the temptation will always be to pray a "certain way," like God isn't capable of hearing or responding to anything else.

I remember every year as a child, we watched Charlton Heston on TV as Moses in *The Ten Commandments*. I still remember the scene where the burning bush and Moses have a conversation. It's a true story told in the Bible.

In the book of Exodus, Moses, after running for his life and hiding on the back side of the desert, gets a visitation from God. God ordered him to go back to Egypt and set the Israelites free. They had been in captivity for centuries. Moses tried to use the excuse that he stuttered and Pharaoh would never listen to him. God responded in Exodus 4:11 by saying, *"Who makes a person's mouth? Who decides whether people speak or do not speak, hear or do not hear, see or do not see? Is it not I, the Lord?"* (NLT)

Now many people talk about this part of the story and say, "See, God can use anyone with any limitations," and that's true. However, think about this for a second: If Moses was a stutterer, wasn't he talking to God that way? He absolutely was!

If you've watched *The Ten Commandments* I know this probably destroys the image of Moses with the polished language of Charlton Heston, but it's true. God was carrying on a conversation with stuttering Moses! If God responded to stuttering Moses, what makes us think that we should be any different? You should talk to God like you would talk to anyone else you have a relationship with, but staying humble enough to revere and respect Him.

Know Who You are Praying To

As we dig a little deeper, I think of two general ground rules that should be in place. The big one is: All praying is done to the Father in the name of Jesus—not to a saint, Mary, or any other person.

John 16:23 (NLT) At that time you won't need to ask me for anything. I tell you the truth, you will ask the Father directly, and he will grant your request because you use my name.

When Jesus said these words, He was referring to the time in which we now live. We are to ask the Father. There are people who pray to

Jesus and that sounds great, doesn't it? The only problem with that is, that is not how Jesus taught us to pray. Jesus can receive our worship and He is giving instruction as the Head of the Church, but all our prayers should go to the Father in the name of Jesus.

The name of Jesus is what allows us to call upon the Father today. Remember, accepting what Jesus did is what gives us access to God, so when we talk to God the Father, it must be in Jesus' name. Therefore, we acknowledge what Jesus has done and the authority His name gives to us.

When we pray to the Father in the name of Jesus, it's just like Jesus standing on the earth talking to the Father. The name of Jesus takes the place of the person of Jesus because He is not here in the flesh. He gave His name to us so we can access the Father the same way He did.

If we are going to pray and get to know God, we can't just address those prayers to "the Big Man upstairs," "the all-knowing God of the universe," or some other name. Jesus taught us by saying, "Our Father" and now we end these prayers to the Father with "in the name of Jesus. Amen."

Believe God is Listening and Will Answer

Let me ask you a question regarding this ground rule of prayer: if you don't believe your prayers are going to be answered, why are you even praying? You *must* believe your effort to talk to God is being honored by Him because He is good and desires to interact with you.

Hebrews 11:6 (NKJV) But without faith it is impossible to please God. For whoever comes to God must believe that He is, and that He

is a rewarder of those who diligently seek Him.

Let's unpack that just a little bit.

First, is God going to answer a prayer with which He isn't pleased? To please Him means we *must* be in faith when we pray. Look again at the middle part of that verse: "*must believe* (have faith) *that He is*." What in the world does that mean?

For many centuries, and even in other translations of the Bible, those words were translated as "must believe that He exists." What good does that do? The Bible tells us that even the demons in hell believe God exists and I'm certain He isn't pleased with them.

So, seriously, what does it mean? Let's go back to stuttering Moses for a second. While having his conversation with God, it takes an interesting turn.

Exodus 3:13–14 (NLT) But Moses protested, "If I go to the people of Israel and tell them, 'The God of your ancestors has sent me to you,' they will ask me, 'What is his name?' Then what should I tell them?" God replied to Moses, "*I am who I am.* Say this to the people of Israel: *I am* has sent me to you."

This doesn't make sense unless you know the whole story of Moses, the children of Israel in Egypt, and the Exodus. God became the very thing Israel needed so they could be set free. Every question Pharaoh had, God became the answer. When God said to Moses, "*I am,*" He was saying, "I am whatever they need me to be." So, if we are going to pray a prayer that pleases God, we *must* first believe He is whatever we need. *He* is the answer everyone is seeking.

The second thing we *must* believe is He is a rewarder. God isn't the stingy kid in the neighborhood who has all the good toys but won't let anyone play with them. God is generous, rewarding, and loves all of humanity! He is ready to reward His children because each believer has fulfilled the rest of what Hebrews 11:6 says. They have sought *Him*.

As Christians, we must believe He isn't going to withhold any good thing from us or make our lives even more miserable so we see what we're missing. God rewards those who seek Him and make Jesus Lord of their life! All praying must be done with this kind of believing.

There is More Than One Kind of Praying

As I said previously, our older son, Preston, was adopted at birth. Our youngest son, Peyton, was as well. Jodi and I enjoy being parents so much and when the opportunity came, quite unexpectedly, to adopt Peyton through a mutual friend in Tulsa, we loved the idea of expanding our family. With the emotional roller-coaster we went through when Preston was born, I didn't know if I had it in me to experience the same events a second time.

I told God I was so honored that this possibility has been brought before me. But I did pray, "You are going to have to protect me this time. I can't go through that emotional stress again." With Preston, we "travailed" (as the old-timers would put it). It was a painful process.

This time we told God we would obey and do whatever we were being led to do, but He would have to work it out. We would do our best to be the best parents to this beautiful boy when he got here, but He would have to make it happen. We met with the aunts of the biological mother, and they loved us. They interviewed us and decided to pick us for the adoption. We were exceptionally happy, but we were waiting to see how things went once Peyton was born (because that's when the wild ride started with Preston).

We gave the situation to God, and oh, how He delivered! Peyton's adoption was as easy as it could have possibly been. I don't remember even feeling fretful. It was a completely different set of circumstances, in a completely different state, and for a completely different child. Nothing was the same, including the stress level!

Peyton was born four days before Preston's birthday, making the week of February 15–20 birthday week at our house. We have a blast starting with Peyton's birthday and finishing with mine. We are Disney, Universal, and Sea World passholders, and that week we are regularly at a different park rocking out for our birthdays. I love celebrating with those two and Jodi every year.

Not only was the situation around their adoptions different, but Peyton and Preston are as different as night and day. Preston is a ham and loves attention. Peyton is shy but still loves a little attention. Preston is submissive and wants to please; Peyton is strong-willed and independent. Both boys are incredibly smart and talented. Peyton does his best to try and be "like bro-er" (which is brother in three-year-old language.) We have two very different blessings from the Lord who require two different kinds of parenting. In the same way, there are different kinds of prayer that function in very different ways.

Ephesians 6:18 says, *"And pray in the Spirit on all occasions with* all kinds of prayers *and requests."* (NIV)

That's a pretty obvious observation, but it's a perfect analogy for what I'm about to tell you: *Prayer is not a grand, general, spiritual tool that can be covered by one set of rules.* There are different kinds of prayer that have different rules. Spiritually speaking, things that apply to one kind of prayer may not apply to the other. If we are going to pray and get our tanks to the half-full mark, we must learn to pray the right way with the right kind of prayer.

I want to briefly explain the different kind of prayer and hopefully direct you to start praying the right prayer for your specific situation. There are amazing books out there that talk about each one of these in detail. but I just want to give you a reference and short description so you can start making real headway in your prayer life.

I do think it's important to note here that God is gracious. I don't believe these rules are something to make someone fearful of "getting it wrong." These are simple guidelines to help on the journey, but nonetheless, this is a journey in which we shouldn't feel any condemnation. Don't be overly concerned about praying the wrong type of prayer when learning to pray. However, as we read before, "the entrance of your Word brings light." (Ps. 119:130) So as we learn to pray the right way, our prayer lives will excel beyond what we have seen, and God will blow our minds.

Asking God for Something

Matthew 21:22 (NLT) You can pray for anything, and if you have faith, you will receive it.

By far, this is the most frequent prayer most people pray. How many times has someone asked for help, healing, blessing, protection, and so much more? This is totally acceptable and should be happening to some degree. As a believer, you can ask God for these things. The rule that applies here is it must be about your desires, needs, or problems. This prayer is someone praying for themselves, not for another person.

In the Old Testament, God made a covenant with Abraham that included protection, financial blessing, healing, and much more. This promise was not just to Abraham, but to all his descendants. In the New Testament, the Bible says if you have a relationship with Jesus, you are part of Abraham's family and those promises belong to you. In short, God is just as interested in people today as He was in the Old Testament. You can ask God for things you need and don't have to let anyone make you feel guilty for asking.

Committing to Do Whatever God Wants You to Do

Luke 22:42 (NLT) "Father, if you are willing, please take this cup of suffering away from me. Yet I want Your will to be done, not mine."

Before Jesus went to the cross, He prayed this prayer. He was making a commitment to follow through completely with what God wanted Him to do. He didn't necessarily want to do it, but He was willing because He had agreed to do it.

This kind of praying isn't to change something; it's a prayer of commitment to God to do something. When you consecrate your life to God to do whatever He wants, you pray this kind of prayer. This is the prayer in which you always pray "if it be Your will." You pray this for specific direction for your life. You pray this when you don't know what that direction may be.

If you are ready to sell out and surrender your will to God, this is the prayer to pray!

Worship

Psalm 22:3 (NLT) Yet you are holy, enthroned (inhabiting) **on the praises of Israel.**

Psalm 95:2 (NLT) Let us come to him with thanksgiving. Let us sing psalms of praise to him.

This is the prayer most people don't see as prayer, but it is. Worship is the very thing that puts you into shared spaced with God. This is the kind of praying where you speak about the greatness of God right to Him. You are telling Him how awesome, great, and majestic He is.

By doing so, you are going right into His very presence. Spiritually speaking, this prayer puts you in the same room with God. Whenever you feel alone, this kind of prayer assures you that will change. Whether you feel Him there or not, this praying puts you there with God. When you pray this prayer, you're speaking what is true about Him and thanking Him for that truth. If you want to spend time with God in His presence, this is how you can get there!

Praying with Someone Else for Something to Happen

Matthew 18:18–20 (NLT) "I tell you the truth, whatever you forbid on earth will be forbidden in Heaven, and whatever you permit on earth will be permitted in Heaven. I also tell you this: If two of you agree here on earth concerning anything you ask, my Father in Heaven will do it for you. For where two or three gather together as my followers, I am there among them."

Of all the prayers we can pray from the Bible, this one is so significant. Look at what part of that verse says, "*My Father in Heaven will do it for you.*" Why is that true? Because at least two people joined together to agree that something would happen. This agreement guarantees it (if it agrees with the Word). When two people come together in His name, He shows up!

When your prayer agrees with just one other believer, you can make all the power of Heaven available. This kind of praying doesn't just double our power in prayer—it multiplies it. You can do 10 times more when you pray in agreement than you can alone. This must be done in complete agreement so it must be decided upon before the praying happens. The person agreeing with you must be praying and believing for the same outcome.

This is the prayer that packs the biggest punch for things to change!

Giving Your Cares to God!

1 Peter 5:7 (AMP) Casting all your cares [all your anxieties, all your worries, and all your concerns, once and for all] on Him, for He cares about you [with deepest affection, and watches over you very carefully).

Most believers don't pray this type of prayer enough. This kind of prayer is what we prayed when our second son, Peyton, was adopted. Often, believers are so upset by what is happening they never turn the situation over to the Lord. The sad thing is they are carrying the problem around when Jesus already carried the problem for them.

This kind of commitment is not committing to God's plan, but committing your cares and problems to the Lord. This prayer will follow asking God for something, because usually what you need causes you to worry and be upset. This prayer reveals what you are going to do with your cares, anxieties, worries, and concerns—give them to God because He isn't going to take them without you giving them to Him. Give those things to Him because, as we said in the last chapter, He is already thinking about it for you!

If you are ready to get rid of some fear, dread, and stress, this is the prayer for you!

The Church Praying Together

Acts 4:23–31 (NLT) As soon as they were freed, Peter and John returned to the other believers and told them what the leading priests and elders had said. When they heard the report, all the believers lifted their voices together in prayer to God: "O Sovereign Lord, Creator of Heaven and earth, the sea, and everything in them—you spoke long ago by the Holy Spirit through our ancestor David, your servant, saying, 'Why were the nations so angry? Why did they waste their time with futile plans? The kings of the earth prepared for battle; the rulers gathered together against the Lord and against his Messiah.' In fact, this has happened here in this very city! For Herod Antipas, Pontius Pilate the governor, the Gentiles, and the people of Israel were all united against Jesus, your holy servant, whom you anointed. But everything they did was determined beforehand according to your will. And now, O Lord, hear their threats, and give us, your servants, great boldness in preaching your word. Stretch out your hand with healing power; may miraculous signs and wonders be done through the name of

your holy servant Jesus." After this prayer, the meeting place shook, and they were all filled with the Holy Spirit. Then they preached the word of God with boldness.

This kind of prayer is the church praying together for the move of God on the earth. Kenneth E. Hagin said, "If it wasn't for times of united prayer in the church, I don't think many of us would be in the body of Christ today." In this kind of prayer, members of the church should be praying with other members that believe like they do.

For the power of God to work in those *outside* the church, Christians must pray *inside* the church. We live in a time where Christians are being persecuted, beheaded, and executed around the world and this type of praying is more important than ever. The Church needs to set aside differences of style, doctrine, and upbringing, and pray for God to save our brothers and sisters. We also need to pray for Christ to be preached across the globe with boldness so the darkness that is trying to overcome will be rolled back and the light of the Gospel will be preached!

All believers, especially local congregations, should be praying together more frequently so those who do not know God can be exposed to God's power and love in their lives and ultimately turn to the God we know.

This is the kind of praying where the people of the Church are praying for the work of the Church to succeed!

To live a full Christian life the way God intended, you must spend time with God regularly. You should be praying regularly to get to know God and to ask Him for something through one of the different types of prayers we discussed. This is another foundational step to becoming a Christian filled with the goodness, power, and perfect love of Christ. This filling allows you to influence the world for God's kingdom.

CHAPTER 10

TAKING COMMUNION

When Jodi and I began dating, the first thing we did was go to dinner together. We went to Chili's on 71st Street near the Woodland Hills Mall in Tulsa, Oklahoma. Over dinner we talked and started the process of getting to know one another. Nearly three hours later we were asked to leave because the restaurant was closing.

There is something about enjoying a meal together that causes walls to come down and a relaxing effect takes place. It was at dinner I began to learn about Jodi's upbringing. She was raised in and around ministry. I learned how her parent's recent divorce had affected her and her sisters. She shared with me the adventure of juggling working for a ministry in town and going to school at Oral Roberts University.

We laughed a lot about the mutual friend who introduced us. I shared a lot about my life, including the spring break story from earlier in the book, the marital problems that my parents were going through at the time, the adventure of being a youth pastor at a small church in a small town, and more.

We talked about the differences of our background. She grew up in Orange County, California. I grew up in Flatwoods, Kentucky. It was like comparing apples to oranges, but we just kept talking and talking and talking. That night went by so effortlessly and so fast.

Our first memories of each other were over a meal. After that, our dating was mostly long distance, but when we were together, we were constantly enjoying meals together. I would cook, she would cook, or we would go out, but the easiest way to relax around each other was at dinner. Communion, also known as "The Lord's Supper," is exactly that.

The story of communion can be found in the four Gospels. It involves the time Jesus took bread and wine and had the Last Supper with his disciples. The Apostle Paul tells a capsulized version of it in 1 Corinthians.

1 Corinthians 11:23–26 (NLT) For I pass on to you what I received from the Lord himself. On the night when he was betrayed, the Lord Jesus took some bread and gave thanks to God for it. Then he broke it in pieces and said, "This is my body, which is given for you. Do this to remember me." In the same way, he took the cup of wine after supper, saying, "This cup is the new covenant between God and his people—an agreement confirmed with my blood. Do this to remember me *as often* as you drink it." For *every time* you eat this

bread and drink this cup, you are announcing the Lord's death until he comes again.

The Last Supper consisted of unleavened bread and wine. It wasn't just a solemn moment with his closest friends before Jesus died. He was doing something very important. It was far more than just the Last Supper. The meal He had with his 12 disciples was the same one known as the "covenant meal."

I know you may be thinking, *what in the world is a covenant?* And even more so, *what is a covenant meal?* Per *Dictionary.com,* a covenant is defined as "an agreement, usually formal, between two or more persons to do or not do something specified." *Encyclopedia Judaica* says concerning a covenant, "Whenever a covenant or contract was established in Bible times, it was confirmed by an oath or solemn meal, or by sacrifices or some other dramatic act like dividing the sacrifices in half and passing or walking through them." Today we sign a piece of paper stating the terms of the agreement and usually we get it notarized to ensure it is official and enforceable.

This was the first act Jesus did with the founding pillars of the church. He was establishing something that would always be a reminder of His death. Communion was going to be a constant reminder of the new contract God was making with man.

What contract was that?

The contract was the agreement with those who would accept what Jesus did. They would enter a relationship with Him and be given an incredible life and future. They would become guilt-free from their sin and be a brand-new person. One day, each of them would do the same thing Jesus did and rise from the dead. They would live forever in Heaven with Him. So, as believers, the partaking of communion is a constant reminder of what He did, and an outward expression of our acceptance of that covenant.

An article in the *Daily Mail* from the United Kingdom quoted a study done by the journal of *Physiology & Behavior*. The report stated that when people enjoyed a meal together, they felt happier and more relaxed, whether at home, work or somewhere else. They felt friendlier, listened more, gave more compliments, and were more likely to make compromises. The people enjoying the meal together believed they were with a warmer and more likeable person and "hierarchies" broke down between bosses and employees and adults and children.

One theory the article presented is that chewing raises serotonin levels in the brain. Serotonin is a chemical in your brain that makes you feel good. It is mostly produced when you sleep, which explains why you feel so bad when you don't sleep.

There is something about enjoying a meal together that causes relationships to grow. Usually tense situations are best handled over a meal. If a friend came to me and showed interest in getting to know a person better, I typically suggest going to lunch or dinner. I believe this was God's intention all along. I believe this is the intention for communion.

The idea of sharing a meal to become closer to someone might be a little unusual to people because they don't understand the biblical idea of communion. Some don't seem to know what it is, but as I have studied relationship building with the Lord over the years I have been in ministry, sharing a meal or communion seems to come up more and more often.

Depending on your upbringing, the idea of communion brings with it a whole lot of different ideas. Some are ritualistic, some include occasional partaking, and some reveal a complete naivety of the topic. Communion is part of our time spent with God and therefore, should be playing a larger role than it is in our walk with God.

It isn't the bread and wine (or juice) that causes any effect on you. You can eat bread and drink wine/juice every day, and it does nothing to fill you up on a spiritual level. It does involve remembering who is behind communion and what He has done for those who partake.

In the Old Testament, when people would eat bread and wine, they were remembering the covenant God made with their forefather, Abraham. Abraham, whose original name was Abram, was a goat herder who God decided to use to build the nation of people that would bring Jesus, the Savior, to the earth. This covenant can be found in Genesis. God originally called Abram and gave him a glimpse of what the covenant would be.

Genesis 12:1–4 (NIV) The Lord had said to Abram, "Go from your country, your people and your father's household to the land I will show you. I will make you into a great nation, and I will bless you; I will make your name great, and you will be a blessing. I will bless those who bless you, and whoever curses you I will curse; and all peoples on earth will be blessed through you." So Abram went, as the Lord had told him; and Lot went with him. Abram was seventy-five years old when he set out from Harran.

Nearly 25 years later, Abram got the details of the agreement.

Genesis 17:1–7 (NIV) When Abram was ninety-nine years old, the Lord appeared to Abram and said to him, "I am Almighty God; walk before Me and be blameless. ***And I will make My covenant between Me and you, and will multiply you exceedingly.*****" Then Abram fell on his face, and God talked with him, saying: "As for Me, behold, My covenant is with you, and you shall be a father of many nations. No longer shall your name be called Abram, but your name shall be Abraham; for I have made you a father of many nations.** ***I will make you exceedingly fruitful; and I will make nations of you, and kings shall come from you. And I will establish My covenant between Me and you and your descendants after you in their generations, for an everlasting covenant, to be God to you and your descendants after you.*****"**

This covenant or agreement would be the basis for everything good that God would do for Abraham and his children after that point in time. Without the agreement, God would not free them from slavery, heal their sick, work any miracles, deliver them from bondage, or anything else. Before He even got the details, Abram agreed to the covenant because He understood the goodness of God. To seal the deal, on faith alone, Abram ate a covenant meal.

Genesis 14:18-20 (NLT) And Melchizedek, the king of Salem and a priest of God Most High, brought Abram some bread and wine. Melchizedek blessed Abram with this blessing: "Blessed be Abram by God Most High, Creator of Heaven and earth. And blessed be God Most High, who has defeated your enemies for you." Then Abram gave Melchizedek a tenth of all the goods he had recovered.

This original agreement was for the Jews, or descendants of Abraham, his son, Isaac, and his grandson, Jacob. This agreement was not big enough for the whole world. Therefore, Jesus came to expand it. When He did, the new agreement included us. Therefore, Jesus' first act with the 12 men who would establish the Church was the same act Abraham did with a character who is only mentioned briefly in the Old Testament—Melchizedek.

Jesus wanted to establish this event as a point of remembrance. The Lord wanted to make this an intimate showing of love He had for us. Every time we partake of communion, we are remembering, in a very intimate way, what Jesus did and how that new agreement of eternal life would be ours.

The bread represents Jesus' body which was beaten, pierced, and broken for all of us. This broken body was a substitute for our body being beaten for the wrong we have done. The wine/juice represents Jesus' blood that was shed for all of us. This blood is what washes away our sins. When we partake in communion, we are partaking in a representation of both the body and blood of Jesus. This is showing, in a physical act, a belief of what we have in our hearts.

When the Apostle John was writing Revelation, the last book of the Bible, He had a vision of Jesus. Jesus spoke to him and told him to write a letter to seven churches. One of those churches was in Ephesus, which was a large city with a megachurch. This is the church Timothy pastored that I mentioned earlier. This church did some amazing things, but the Lord still had a problem with them.

Revelation 2:2–5 (NIV) I know your deeds, your hard work and your

perseverance. I know that you cannot tolerate wicked people, that you have tested those who claim to be apostles but are not, and have found them false. You have persevered and have endured hardships for my name, and have not grown weary. Yet I hold this against you: You have *forsaken the love you had at first.* Consider how far you have fallen! Repent and do the *things you did at first.* If you do not repent, I will come to you and remove your lampstand from its place. (More to come on the lampstand shortly.)

Look at all the wonderful things this church was doing. They ministered to wicked people, exposed false preachers, protected the flock, suffered persecution because they were Christians, and they didn't give up. Considering all the good they were doing, they still had a problem. What would kind of problem would a church like that have?

Let me explain something before we dig into this church's problem. Many people get scared of looking at the Bible in any other way than the Bible they buy in the store. It is common knowledge that the Bible was not written in English, but rather in Hebrew and Greek. Sometimes the English language doesn't convey the full weight of the original Greek and Hebrew, so it is beneficial to go back and look at the original writing and see what the original words meant.

In the Greek language, the words from Revelation 2:4, "*love you had at first,*" ("first love" in other translations) are the words "protos agape." Now let's look at these two words. "Protos" means "above all, in supremacy." The word "agape" is mostly the Greek word "love," but here, according to *Enhanced Strong's Lexicon*, it is translated "love feast." The church at Ephesus had stopped partaking in the "love feast" or communion.

Because of this, the Bible said their lampstand was going to be removed from its place. This seems to be an unusual statement to us today. What difference would it make to remove their lampstand?

In Bible times, obviously, no one had electricity, so to see at night, they had to have an open-flame lamp, like a camping lantern. Much like a lantern, a lamp was something that had oil in it, and many times in Scripture, oil was a reference to the Holy Spirit.

What God was saying to the church in Ephesus was they had stopped doing the first act Jesus established. They allowed Jesus' actions to be pushed out of their thoughts and replaced them with the work of being Christians and a church. *Running the church had become more important than the very reason the church existed.*

Because of this lack of giving communion the premiere place in the life of the church, God was telling them the Holy Spirit would be removed from their church. This was going to happen, not because communion was a ritual, but because it was something meant to *constantly show and remind them of what Jesus had done for the church,* as well as what they had accepted from Him. Without constantly staying in remembrance of what Jesus did, everything else was a waste of time. They had gotten away from the intimacy that comes from regular communion. They had gotten into the business of church, but had *forgotten the passion* of a relationship with Jesus.

This was a pattern for every member of the Early Church, and that is what believers should be doing today. Not in a religious way, but because of a passionate remembrance of what Jesus did when He suffered and died for all.

Acts 2:42 (NLT) All the believers devoted themselves to the apostles' teaching, and to fellowship, and *to sharing in meals (including the Lord's Supper)*, and to prayer.

Why is communion so important? Is drinking wine/juice and eating bread that essential to the lives and development of a believer? Again, in and of themselves, they aren't that important. There are millions of people that partake of communion with no understanding, and they miss the heart behind it. Without the heart that accompanies it, communion is just an empty act. However, in the book of 1 Corinthians, we see a little clearer understanding of what communion includes.

1 Corinthians 10:16 (NKJV) The cup of blessing which we bless, is it not the *communion* of the blood of Christ? The bread which we break, is it not the *communion* of the body of Christ?

1 Corinthians 1:9 (NKJV) God is faithful, by whom you were called into the *fellowship* of His Son, Jesus Christ our Lord.

This word communion and this word fellowship are the same Greek word—koinonia. What an unusual word. It is one we don't often use today. This word, even though it is foreign to us who speak English, means "intimacy."

Communion was one of the focal points of the Early Church because it created intimacy between the Church and the Lord. It created a heart of remembrance within each believer of everything Jesus did. Communion does the same for believers today. It creates a strong remembrance in everyone who partakes in it.

We are reminded of the breaking of His body and shedding of

His blood so we could have access to God. He paid for our guilt, removed it, and makes us a new person. Every time we partake of communion, it shouldn't be looked at as a religious ritual, but as a reminder. Communion causes the love we have for God to grow. It seals our relationship with Him.

When Jesus rose from the dead, He appeared to two of the disciples. They didn't recognize Him at all. He spoke with them and expounded on Scripture. He explained things very thoroughly, but they still didn't recognize Him. Luke tells us that something happened, and suddenly they could recognize Him.

Luke 24:30–31 (NLT) As they sat down to eat, He took the bread and blessed it. Then He broke it and gave it to them. Suddenly, their eyes were opened, and they recognized Him. And at that moment He disappeared!

It wasn't until Jesus broke the bread that they recognized who He was. I believe it's because they understood what that covenant meal represented. They couldn't help but think about Him and when He broke bread for them the last time.

Communion is being intimate with the Lord. Communion is enjoying the very thing, in a spiritual sense, that sets us free and fills us up with His presence.

The Old Testament refers to communion also.

Exodus 25:30 (NLT) "Place the Bread of the Presence on the table to remain before me at all times."

The words "bread of presence" are the Hebrew word "paneh,"

which means “the face,” but it comes from the root word “panah” which means to “face the appearance or the presence of God.”

The Old Testament priests were ordered to gather once a week at the tabernacle. The tabernacle was where the presence of God dwelled. The tabernacle was made from tent-like material. It was the place where everyone in the country of Israel communed with God. They later changed to a permanent and elaborately constructed temple which was envisioned by King David and built by his son, King Solomon.

The priests were ordered to meet and eat the bread that was placed on the inner furniture. One piece of furniture was called the Table of Showbread, or the “bread of presence.” At that stage in history, God didn’t live in anyone’s heart. His presence was only accessible by certain people who were empowered to be in His presence.

These priests took care of the tabernacle, and later the temple, offered sacrifices to cover everyone’s sin, and carried the pieces of the tabernacle to the next location. They set up the tabernacle and made sure it was perfect. It’s like a new church that is portable and sets up its furniture, stage, and sound system every week at a location and then tears everything down when church is dismissed. (We know that feeling well as we did this for a season when we started Direction Church.)

When the priests came to eat the bread, they were also burning frankincense as a sweet-smelling aroma to the Lord. They were enjoying a covenant meal and ministering to the Lord. Eating the showbread in the Hebrew meant they were literally experiencing the presence of God.

Personal Application

Now that we have a better understanding of what communion is all about, let's talk about how it applies to your life now. It seems as if I am encouraging the act of communion alone. Let me emphasize that taking the bread and wine/juice does nothing for anyone in and of itself. It is the heart behind communion. However, it is the very act that puts someone into that state of mind.

Intimacy in a marital relationship is a physical act that connects the heart of the husband to the heart of his wife. It is a physical show of a heart-felt love. In a sense, this is also what partaking of communion truly means. It is a physical show of a heart-felt love. Paul said, "*As often as you eat this bread and drink this cup, you proclaim the Lord's death till He comes.*" (1 Corinthians 11:26, NKJV)

When someone takes communion in a religious and non-heartfelt manner—out of obligation or duty—they are having empty intimacy with God. Counselor's offices are filled with couples that are having intimacy issues across the world. They say the intimacy in their relationship is unfulfilling and cold. They state that intimacy is done almost out of obligation, not out of love.

This is the single most important factor in the taking of communion. It should never be looked upon as an act alone. It is a physical act that should always be tied to your heart. Paul tells us how important this is.

1 Corinthians 11:27–30 (NLT) So anyone who eats this bread or drinks this cup of the Lord unworthily is guilty of sinning against the body and blood of the Lord. *That is why you should examine yourself*

***before eating the bread and drinking the cup*. For if you eat the bread or drink the cup without honoring the body of Christ, you are eating and drinking God's judgment upon yourself. That is why many of you are weak and sick and some have even died.**

The word "unworthily" is the Greek word "anaxious," which means "irreverently." In the Corinthian church, people were drinking the communion wine to get drunk and eating the bread for regular food. So, what was Paul telling them in those verses? He was saying the way they were taking it was wrong. He was telling them communion could not and would not do anything for them. He was saying communion must be taken in a way that our hearts had to be in the right state of love and appreciation for what Jesus had done for us.

It is in this way that communion brings you closer to God. You are in His presence while receiving it. Consistently partaking in communion will keep your heart right and bring things to the surface in your life which need to be confronted and conquered. This is not because the bread and wine/juice contain some magical power by themselves, but your remembrance and heartfelt love—when coupled with your faith and soul-searching—allow you to enter an intimate act with the Lord and grow closer to Him. How can you spend that kind of time with the Lord and not see areas of your life that need to change?

"How Often Should I Partake?"

A lot of churches, including ours, offer church communion once a month. I'm not here to condemn that practice because I understand, as a pastor, the constant preparation work that goes into it and churches have so many other responsibilities and needs to address. This book isn't written to churches as much as it is written to you as an individual believer!

How intimate are you being if you partake in communion once a month? My recommendation is take communion as often as you think about it. In a marriage, how good is it if there is only intimacy once a month? The same thing applies in your relationship with Jesus. How good can your relationship with Him be if you hardly ever think about what He did for you?

If you rarely or never come face to face with Him and the knowledge of what He did for you, your relationship is not as it should be. If you never think about His body that was broken for you or His blood that was shed for you, how can you be filled the way God intended? *Communion is specific to the actions of Jesus' death. You can't help but think about what He did when you partake of it.*

If you consider these spiritual truths about communion with the discoveries I presented in the beginning of the chapter, you can begin to see how something that has been looked at as ritualistic has been downplayed! We have been missing a great benefit when it comes to living a full Christian life!

¾ Mark: Regularly Attending and Being Involved in Local Church

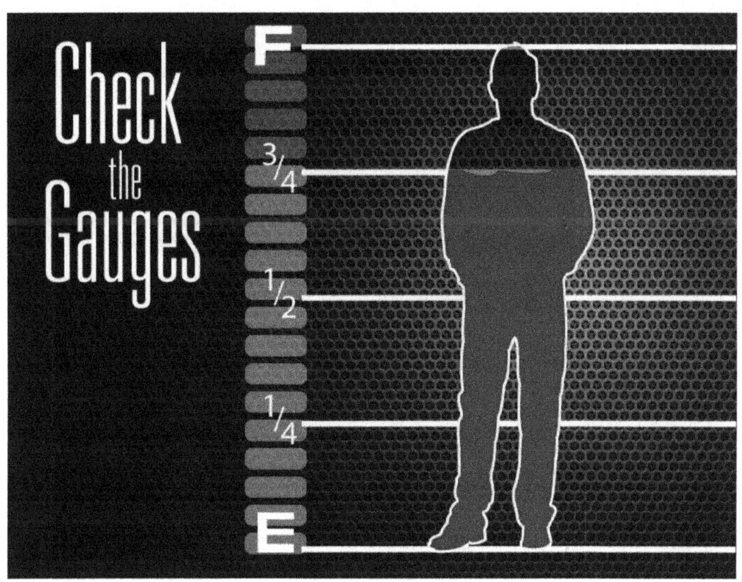

Chapter 11

Every Christian Needs to be Involved in Church

I grew up as an only child. My mom and dad decided that having one child was enough, and since they got it perfect the first time, why try again? (Don't roll your eyes at me! Ha-ha!) Since I had no brothers and sisters, my appreciation for cousins was huge. Even though my immediate family consisted of just the three of us, my extended family was enormous. My dad has four siblings and my mom has two. In addition, my grandparents on both sides were very close to their siblings. So, on both sides of the family, there were literally 50 to 60 cousins that I saw every holiday, and many of them every Sunday eating lunch at my grandmother's house.

I also lived next door to a pair of cousins and rode to school with them every day. In the small town of Flatwoods, Kentucky, you're never too far from a family member. I loved every holiday, reunion, birthday, and get-together. The closeness of a family that large was something I still treasure to this day. It meant the world to have family there to laugh, play, celebrate, and enjoy. Some of these cousins were as close as siblings because we stayed at each other's homes so frequently.

I remember one year, my cousin Sean and I spent almost an entire summer at his house or mine. In those two-and-a-half months of summer break, we got a little tired of each other. However, we had been to Florida, numerous fairs, seen tons of fireworks shows, played a lot of ATARI, watched 1,000 movies, rode what seemed like 10,000 miles on our bikes, and literally wore out our welcome. What a great summer that was!

Other members, even though they lived in other states, were even more special when they would come home. My parents and I lived next door to my grandparents and my dad's sister and her family. I remember sitting in front of my grandparent's house waiting on our out-of-state family to drive in from Virginia. We lived on a large hill that overlooks the city. You can see for miles and can see all of Reed Street as it snakes its way to our driveway. It meant so much when I saw that little black Chevette make the turn and come up the hill. I knew that the next few days or week was going to be epic. The fun we would have was second to none!

The other thing that meant so much during these wonderful times was not just the play, but the enjoyment and exchange of love and smiles. We would sit around the table with our parents and our grandparents. We'd tell stories, laugh, and eat.

Whenever someone on either side of the family faced a crisis, they never felt like they were facing it alone. It was more like everyone felt what you felt, faced what you faced, and prayed for you, as you would pray for yourself.

In 1977, my mom was diagnosed with a blood disease called pemphigus that almost killed her. I was in first grade and barely saw my mom during the whole school year. They would sneak me into her hospital room occasionally, but I remember staying at my grandparents most of the time. However, when I look back, the situation never seemed weird or out of the ordinary because we always seemed to spend so much time there anyway.

Both of my grandmothers would read children's books with me, watch television with me, and cook awesome meals for me. My uncle, who was still in high school, would watch *Star Trek* and *Doctor Who* with me, as well as my favorite cartoons. Papaw would watch *The Dukes of Hazard* and make me feel as if I were the most special kid in the world. I'm sure all my cousins could tell you he said this to them too, but he was a master at making you feel so important. He would say, "Heeeeeeeey! There's my boy and I wouldn't take ten million dollars for him!" Then he would hug me, and I knew he meant it.

While my parents were at the hospital, I was shielded from the severity and everything was just as regular and comfortable as could be. I didn't know until much later how severe my mom's sickness was. There was no cure for her illness, and the doctors knew very little about it at that time.

But the other thing that our family was doing together was calling family prayer meetings specifically for my mom and what she was facing. They were praying for her and asking God to heal her. This was happening on a regular basis because they were with us in the fight. They were facing it with us, believing with us, and expecting God to heal my mom right along with us. To use a church phrase, they were "agreeing with us for her healing." What a huge impact a close-knit family plays on the people we become!

In much the same way, this is what the Church is for every believer. It is a family to belong to, agree in prayer with, and grow up physically and spiritually with!

Most of the time, when people think of going to and being part of a church, there are two extremes that come to their minds. The first extreme is they replace a personal relationship with God with a relationship with the church. They have the attitude that if anyone thinks they can have a personal relationship with God *outside* the church, they are on dangerous ground. This school of thought teaches extreme dependence on the Church. But this way of thinking is *very* wrong! God decided to live in the hearts of believers, not in a building built by humans anymore. If God lives in your heart, you have full access to Him without anyone else talking to Him for you. In fact, as believers, Jesus already did the talking for us, and if we need more talking in the future, He will do that too.

1 John 2:1 (NIV) My dear children, I write this to you so that you will not sin. But if anyone does sin, we have an advocate (One who talks for us and pleads our case) **with the Father—Jesus Christ, the Righteous One.**

The second extreme is the "I-don't-need-church-at-all" people. These people hardly ever darken the doorstep of the Church; or they cruise around from church to church, going wherever they feel is "the place" this week. They believe they can just pray and read their Bible and go their own way, all alone, wherever and however they feel. That school of thought is wrong too.

Of course, as the first two sections of this book explained, there is the greatest benefit that comes from reading your Bible and praying. It will cause you to grow, and you will experience some infilling of God's Spirit, but that is only half of the tank. *God will always lead you to someone else so they can speak into your life a word or expose you to a side of God you can't experience on your own and both will bring assistance and help to you.* The words "assistance" or "help" don't mean they are doing something *for* you; it means they are making something easier to do.

Paul made a very similar statement when he said the following:

1 Corinthians 11:1 (NLT) Follow my example as I follow the example of Christ.

Jesus said something along the same lines when He was talking about someone else assisting us into His presence.

Matthew 18:20 (NLT) For where two or three gather in My name, there am I with them.

The proper place for the Church to have in our journey to a full Christian life can be summed up in this statement: *There is a side of God you are never going to understand or experience unless you have regular fellowship with other members of the body of Christ.* When I say the body of Christ, I am talking about other Christians. The Church is the place where experiences and communication with other members is supposed to happen on a regular basis.

Hebrews 10:24–25 (NLT) Let us think of ways to motivate one another to acts of love and good works. And let us not neglect our meeting together, as some people do, but encourage one another, especially now that the day of His return is drawing near.

The writer of the book of Hebrews is putting a real challenge on us as believers. He is telling us that, of course, we should motivate each other to keep up the good work. The best way to motivate ourselves to keep living for God—or to get filled to the next level—is by regularly meeting with each other. What is he saying? To build relationships with other Christians that the believer goes to church with!

A lot of people read that and agree they need relationships with the body of Christ, but don't want to or will not join a local congregation. They believe floating from church to church is the answer. They think that if they float from church to church, then they can fellowship with the whole body of Christ. What a shortsighted point of view.

Real, meaningful, life-giving, and life-changing relationships are not built from casual meetings from time to time. The more time a person puts in with someone, the stronger the relationship grows. Look at what happened when Peter and John were released from prison.

Acts 4:23 (NIV) On their release, Peter and John went back to *their own people* and reported all that the chief priests and the elders had said to them.

When they needed comfort, encouragement, help and advice, they didn't just grab someone they barely knew. They jumped into the middle of the infant church in Jerusalem, which included people they had spent time with. The relationships they had with those people were real and genuine. Those relationships had been bathed in time.

When people do not join the church, they are missing out on life-changing relationships. The local church's strength is this kind of relationship. If it was permissible to go from one church to another, why did the apostles go through the trouble of starting local churches in the first place? These local churches were not established by the apostles (or today by people who felt called of God) to be like a drive-in movie theater. They were built to become a home where believers could become family, grow together, and develop life-giving, life-changing relationships.

These relationships strengthen you, as a believer, in two ways. The first way is by what those relationships can do for you. There is much to be said about the people you sit next to in church every week. There are people that have means, resources, experiences, knowledge, and other answers to prayer about which you have no idea. God can use someone that surprises you.

I remember the first time someone from our church gave a large donation. It was humbling because I didn't expect God to use them that way. It was only because of the relationship I had with them that opened the door, unknowingly to me, for them to help us accomplish what God was calling us to do.

Although that was a huge blessing to me, don't be fooled into limiting help to strictly financial. The real strength of the body of Christ is what they can do for each other in various ways! If someone knows something I don't know and shares it with me, they've helped me. If someone gives me advice, they've helped me. If someone who knows how to pray down Heaven prays for me, they've helped me. People in the church can help each other in ways you would never guess.

There is a story of a pastor who was sitting in his office one day when an elderly lady walked in and said, "Pastor, I just wanted you to know that I am retiring and moving to Florida, and you'll want to find someone to take over for me." The pastor laughed and congratulated her. She had been a friendly lady who had come to the church ever since he had been the pastor. She never seemed to get overly involved, but she was always there, saying amen when he preached. He then looked at her and said, "What area do we need to get a replacement for you in?" To his surprise, she responded, "I've prayed for you every day, early in the morning and late at night, since the day you became the pastor of this church. I don't want to see what God is doing in you change or let down, so please find someone else to pray for you because I'll be moving away." After she left, the pastor laid his head on his desk and cried because he realized the success he had enjoyed had not just come from his hard work, but from what the body of Christ was doing for each other, including what they were doing for him.

The second way being a part of a church helps a believer to be filled is the exact opposite from the first. It is what *you* can do for someone else or for the church itself. What you do for someone else will also strengthen you as well. When you do something for someone else, you are making room for more of that in your life!

Luke 6:38 (NLT) Give, and you will receive. *Your gift will return to*

***you in full*—pressed down, shaken together to make room for more, running over, and poured into your lap. The amount you give will determine the amount you get back.**

In short, this verse promises that whatever you are giving out will cause more of that to come back into your life. When you sow help, you will receive help; when you sow resources, you will receive resources; when you sow good things to someone else, you will receive the same in return.

A Lesson from Late Night—Why Church is So Important

"And now ladies and gentlemen, heeeeeeeeeeeere's Johnny!" For those who know exactly what that saying is all about, you are no doubt fans of late night TV. I grew up not getting to watch Johnny Carson because he was on past my bedtime. However, I was old enough to remember the late-night wars.

After Johnny Carson retired, David Letterman and Jay Leno both battled for the most coveted spot at 11:30 p.m. Leno won the slot on NBC with Letterman going to CBS and splintering the country's viewing that had solely belonged to Johnny. That was when I became a big fan of late night talk shows. Even though I was a supporter of Letterman's show because I more identified with his sense of humor, I was very excited for Jimmy Fallon when he took Leno's place on *The Tonight Show*. He is a good interviewer, very funny, and came with some of the best writers in the business. The creativity of the show is what set *The Tonight Show* apart when he became the host.

One of my favorite segments he did on his show *Late Night with Jimmy Fallon* before coming to *The Tonight Show* was called "Audience

Shared Experiences." This popular segment had the audience participate together in a random, usually funny event; hilarious things like everyone shooting nerf darts at an actor who is quietly playing Jenga; the entire audience releasing an untied, fully inflated balloon at the same moment just to see where they went; every member dressing up like the cast of *Jersey Shore*; and the list of shared experiences went on and on. These were shared experiences that people watching, and certainly people in the audience, would always remember for the rest of their lives.

Jimmy was not alone in creating these experiences. In New York City, there is an improvisational troop called "Improv Everywhere." This eclectic group of actors, comics, and fun-loving individuals create similar shared experiences, out in public, for all to see. In 2012 on Black Friday they formed a waiting line in front of a $.99 store with a bunch of actors going in to "shop" for amazing deals. They also have taken a troop of actors dressed in blue shirts and khaki pants to a Best Buy and just stood around. "The no-pants subway ride," the "high five on the escalator," "frozen grand central," and "reverse times square," are just a few of their stunts that create hilarious shared experiences. (Go ahead. Look them up on YouTube. I'll wait. But promise you'll come back.)

These events have the sole purpose of creating an experience that people will share at the time and for the rest of their lives in memory. These experiences are not just shared by those who are participating, but also for those watching it happen.

A flash mob is a group of people who assemble suddenly in a public place, perform an unusual and seemingly pointless act for a brief time, then quickly disperse, often for the purposes of entertainment, satire, and artistic expression. Many times, they are sending a message, but other times they are just being funny. It's all about the experience at the time.

I know many people think, "*Those people need to get a life,*" but I want to challenge you with this thought: what if the power of each other sharing a common experience *is* the life those people need to get? Shared experiences tie people together, develop relationships, and make us who we are. The reality is our culture is starving for them. Why is that?

Shared experiences can be defined as "events in life that people encounter, live through, or do together." Shared experiences aren't anything new. I mentioned earlier about family gatherings or company coming over. These were shared experiences. For decades, evening television viewing has been a gigantic shared experience. Even back to the days of radio, families would sit down after dinner, and with millions of other people, would share the experience of their favorite show, and then they would talk about it after it was over. The evidence was in the next day at work. People have conversations around the water cooler or coffee pot discussing what they watched the night before. They would stand around and talk until the boss came and corralled everyone back to work.

We can go back even further before television and radio to the days when people had to go to a theater or the coliseum for entertainment. People dressed up and went out and interacted with one another at the show, gladiator event, concert, bull fights, and even church. Those experiences strengthened the fabric of our relationships with each other. It was accepted as a part of life.

Try to remember back to a major world event that happened in your lifetime. Think about things specific to your area of the world (or your life) for example: when your favorite sports team won their last championship, a loved one passed away, you got a raise, or an overtly funny moment. You can probably remember where you were and I'm willing to guess you could tell me if you were alone or not and most likely who you were with. Even if you can't remember who it was, you'll say something like, "Someone was with me because I said to them…"

If this has been happening for a while, and many people can share a lot of the same memories that I do, what's the big deal? Here it is: Shared experiences are still very popular today, but they aren't the same. People still go to work, go to the movies, go out and about and so on, but what has changed is an alarming number of people who will come in, not talk to anyone in the office, arena, cinema or store, except for the standards of "Hello" or "Good morning," and get out as quickly as possible to head back to their "cocoon."

People sit in the same room and text each another. Kids will sit in the same room with their families with headphones in while texting, doing homework, watching a YouTube video, posting to Instagram and Snapchat. The whole thing might be broadcast on Facebook Live or Periscope. The parents are equally as guilty while sitting in the same room updating their own Facebook, checking their work email, posting pictures of their dinner or the sunset (or both), and nobody is talking.

We have substituted genuine shared experiences that happened naturally for ones we must foster. I believe it's because we don't share life together like we used to. Families are splintering, the economy has forced people to move to other parts of the country or the world to survive financially, and people have become so focused on their career that many are raising a generation of socially lopsided people who desperately need a sense of community that the world has less and less of. It is the genuine shared experience of living life together in communities that makes people whole.

Some of the greatest tools created to improve human being's productivity, have produced side effects in how people interact with one another. I am not one of these people who love/hate modern technology or modern communication methods, but I do want to point out how much people have used them as a substitute for actual physical interaction. Everything from answering machines and voicemail, to email, to social media has caused people to interact with one another less and less in person.

I've called someone hoping to just leave a voicemail and was so shocked (and a little disappointed) when the person answered the phone. I didn't know what to say. I have sent emails to people to avoid a lengthy conversation. I believe in technology and the next "big thing." However, the original "big thing" was *each other* and there is no substituting that.

You can't become a well-rounded person without sharing life with other people. You can't become the fullest version of yourself without regular fellowship with other believers. The more the merrier! We need to, once again, experience the power of being not just *around,* but with each other. Phones, tablets, and all other electronics turned off.

This is what belonging to a church does for us. The world is starving for interaction without realizing how much they are starving. God, in his ultimate goodness, created us that way and created a way for us to receive it. He designed the Church!

How Did the World Become So Hungry?

The change in America happened during the Industrial Revolution. Up until that time, the home was not just a place to sleep and eat, but was also the place that most of the social interaction took place. The members of the family solved problems together, worked the farm together, and enjoyed one another. People who lived in rural communities began moving to cities for greater financial income and a greater chance at the "American Dream." They left the farms to go work in factories.

Until then, they lived close by families and knew everyone in their small towns. You would think that moving closer to a denser population would cause a social circle to grow, but the opposite happened. Instead of knowing everyone, having a highly-localized upbringing and well-rounded set of family and town values, the young families broke off to explore their own paths and pick influences from fewer and fewer people, some from people they didn't even know. By separating themselves from a larger group of strong influences in a smaller community to a smaller group of strong influences in a larger community, they made things lopsided and people have been less and less social ever since.

Strong Relationships Were God's Original Intention

God's intention all along was for people to experience more of Him through each other. He never created anyone to be alone in their walk with Him. I have heard it said by some people who are trying to sound spiritual that they don't *need* anyone. "I just *need* Jesus," or "God is all I *need*." We have even sung it in church. The lyrics to a very beautiful song "All I need. All I need. Jesus, you're all I need."

I understand the thought behind the song, and to have a relationship with God, that is true. Nobody else but Jesus Christ can give you the relationship with God that everyone must have. It is through His Son that a relationship with God comes, but God didn't design us to only have a relationship with Him. If we look back when God created everything, He did something much different than what we would expect.

Genesis 2:18 (NLT) The Lord God said, "It is not good for the *man to be alone*. I will make a helper suitable for him.

As discussed more than once in earlier chapters, Adam was very close to God in a way nobody else has been. It was in that relationship God said the words we just read. I believe God created us from the very beginning to experience each other as well as Him.

Let's look again at what the book of Hebrews says.

Hebrews 10:24–25 (NLT) Let us think of ways to *motivate one another to acts of love and good works. And let us not neglect our meeting together*, as some people do, *but encourage one another*, especially now that the day of his return is drawing near.

Is the Bible telling believers why there is a need for strong relationships inside the church? Is it to benefit mankind? Yes! The sad thing is many have started to remove themselves from being around others and, by doing so, have robbed themselves of social and spiritual maturity and a well-rounded view of who God is.

Animals that travel in herds understand this without explanation.

When a water buffalo or wildebeest separate from the pack, they are asking to get attacked by the lion. Try and tell a herd animal they don't need the herd. They all need the herd to survive. *So do believers!* In addition to a divine relationship with the Creator, God designed everyone to have relationships with other people.

Why is that? Because inside each of us is a little piece of God and without each other, we may never discover that part of God.

Genesis 2:7 (NKJV) And the Lord God formed man of the dust of the ground, and breathed into his nostrils the breath of life; and man became a living being.

The very breath of God. Think about that. God's breath came from Him and that's what gives us life. Our spirit is a little piece of God because all things created came from Him. If we all have a small piece of God inside of us (and those who are born again actually have had that piece come alive), then those living pieces inside us, and others, are one way He reveals Himself more and more. God's original intention was for Adam to experience more of who God was by Him pouring a different part of Himself into Eve than He poured into Adam. That's why people are so different. Humanity, or even all of creation, has yet to contain everything God is, but every person represents more of God's image than what one person can ever contain on their own.

I think it's important to mention here that I am not for one second saying everything about everyone is an example of the image of God. I believe everyone has areas that need sanctification, and we all have areas of weakness that need to be worked on. However, the part in every believer that's born again and growing *is* a part of Him that other believers should be experiencing. Some part of God that a believer may never achieve or grow into on their own may be experienced from someone else. The power of Christian relationships will show believers more of God's character.

I remember learning and experiencing a lot of what I know about God through interaction with someone else. A lesson from my Sunday school teacher, one of my pastor's powerful sermons, the evangelist's illustration at youth camp, my professors in Bible college, the testimony from someone I know, or even just a conversation with a good friend about the goodness of God. These examples are things that have shown a side of God to me that was something I had not noticed on my own. That interaction, however, is not a substitute for what reading the Word and spending time with God will get me on my own. Allowing others to speak into our lives is a supplemental way to keep what we receive on our own well-rounded. It is the revelation we would never achieve on our own that comes from the peace of God found inside someone else. Others broaden our understanding and bring more light than we can achieve on our own. This was God's original intention. Adam would have never known about the reproducing side of God without Eve.

For reasons people have not understood, shared experiences have always been loved and craved. From the earliest days after Adam and Eve's garden, to the Tower of Babel, to the gladiator days, to the Greeks with the creation of the Olympics and schools, to the invention of modern sports, to nightclubs and social spots, to chat rooms, to long distance phone calls, to video calling, mankind has been, and very much is, a social race of beings that love being together.

Men build stadiums, coliseums, and giant gathering places.

(There is a place in Lagos, Nigeria that seats 2,000,000 people under one roof in a building that is one mile long and half a mile wide.) Inside these arenas, they place giant interactive scoreboards and video screens because just being there isn't enough. They want to intensify the experience so they make it even more tangible so people can share the experience more intensely. They have also built theme parks that can handle hundreds of thousands of people at a time. Inside those venues are activities, game rooms, rides, and thousands of ways to make the giant shared experience more specific.

More than 100 years ago, when people absolutely couldn't be together, they sent things via Pony Express. Later they invented the telegraph, telephone, text messaging, and web cameras. People have parties, social mixers, conferences, seminars, and meetings. These are ways people scratched the itch of the need for shared experiences. Therefore, people have begun fostering more shared experiences on top of daily shared experiences.

Imagine going to a baseball game where thousands of people are already going to be there. The team and the ballpark want to make an even more special shared experience, so "the first 850 fans get a free bobblehead figure." Or imagine going to a neighborhood park where lots of people will be and seeing people dancing to music only them and their friends can hear because they are listening to the same song with their ear buds in. How about taking someone's kids to a crowded mall to ride the virtual roller coaster or carousel with their friends. Even some people who like slower paced events will go with their friends just to people-watch. These are man-made shared experiences and all the participants are tied together by that one experience, even if they never meet each other again. Those bobbleheads they received, pictures they may have taken, videos they posted to their social media pages, or even just the memories of the day ensure that bonding together from that experience forever.

The thing that's disturbing is that kind of social interaction is being done less and less in the real world with each other and more and more online. Society is starving for shared experiences with other people and yet those same people are staying under their safety blanket and being anti-social by jumping online. Society has substituted virtual interaction for actual interaction and I believe that is why fostering shared experiences has become so popular.

I remember when I was six years old and Elvis died. My mom sat in front of the TV with an audio cassette recorder and recorded his last concert. We sat in awe as "The King" wowed an audience of 18,000. That night was an incredible thing to see on television and we shared it with millions of other viewers. In fact, if you were alive then, you may remember that. That memory ties us together, but that is just on one dimension. We saw it on television. That amazing event did not begin to compare to my first live concert. I was one of 12,000 people packed into the Charleston Civic Center in Charleston, West Virginia to see the surviving members of Lynyrd Skynyrd. Even though they weren't Elvis—for that matter they weren't even Skynyrd, but what was left after the plane crash—that didn't matter. The experience blew me away! To see 12,000 fans interact with them was incredible. All 12,000 of us were bonded by the venue, the sights, the sound, the response to the band, the lighting, the pyrotechnics, and the emotion. We connected and shared an experience on multiple levels.

Similarly, the first time I walked into Rupp Arena to see the Kentucky Wildcats play basketball was a mind-numbing experience. You must understand that for a boy who grew up in Kentucky, Rupp Arena is our Yankee Stadium, Fenway Park, Texas Stadium, Wrigley Field, South Bend with "Touchdown Jesus," Dodger Stadium, or Candlestick Park all rolled in to one. The largest college basketball arena in the country was sold out with 23,000+ screaming fans to see them play a "nobody." That event was so incredible, I will never forget it. I am forever tied to the people from the Skynyrd concert and from Rupp Arena because of our shared experience.

This was God's original intention for humanity. So, what better place is there to experience His intention than in His house—the local church? If you don't join a church to regularly experience the piece of God in members of your church family, you will be lopsided and not as well-rounded as you could be.

There Is *Real* Power in Church Relationships

(I'd like to add a short disclaimer here. I don't claim to know everything in the mind of God in this book. I'm just writing some things down I believe God showed me. If you choose not to accept what I am saying, that's okay. I pray God shows you in a way that clicks in your understanding and you grow closer to Him through it. Now, back to your regularly scheduled program. Ha-ha!)

If God's original intent was for us to have the shared experience of church, what was He thinking? The first thing I believe is important to understand is there is *real power* in shared church experiences. Why is that? Let's look at a completely natural, scientific study and remove the spiritual aspect for just a brief period here.

Dr. Rollin McCraty, Director of Research of the HeartMath Research Center at the Institute of HeartMath in Boulder Creek, California, wrote an article entitled "The Electricity of Touch: Detection and Measurement of Cardiac Energy Exchange Between People." In it he wrote the following:

"We present a sampling of results which provide intriguing evidence that *an exchange of electromagnetic energy produced by the heart occurs when people touch or are in proximity.* One's Electrocardiogram (ECG) (heart activity) signal is registered in another person's electroencephalogram (EEG) (brain activity) and elsewhere on the other person's body. While this signal is strongest when people are in contact, it is still detectable when subjects are in proximity without contact.

"This study represents one of the first successful attempts to directly measure exchanged energy between people and provides a solid, testable theory to explain the observed effects of many healing modalities that are based upon the assumption that an energy exchange takes place."

So, that's a whole lot of fancy science jargon, isn't it? Well, to use terminology we all understand, Dr. McCraty took two people in three different experiments. In one, he sat them next to each other and had them hold hands. In another, they sat back to back not holding hands. In the third, they sat in close-proximity not touching at all. In these tests, he could then detect the heart rate of one person in the other person's brain waves. There was energy, that was measurable, being transferred between people.

Think about any time someone yawns. A few seconds later, if someone else is close and sees it, they too will yawn. A group of people laughing at a restaurant might find an outsider who may be watching them smiling without realizing it. When someone experiences a death, they usually surround themselves with other loved ones. The power of being around others comforts them and strengthens them to make it through, even without talking about it. The mere presence of family and friends makes things better. Close friends and family seem to just "know" something is not right even though no one is saying anything. This study, I believe, makes a whole lot of sense for those things happening. Energy is being exchanged between people all the time whether they realize it or not.

Now, let's bring it back to the spiritual. This study is truly fascinating and exciting to hear, but I believe it is a confirmation of God's original intent and was confirmed by Jesus. The reason people need a church family is all of humanity strengthens each other and affects one another by an exchange of power. Human bodies were designed for the exchange to take place.

Mark 16:18b (NIV) They will place their hands on sick people, and they will get well.

We understand God's power is what does the healing. But God created our bodies to be a conduit His power can flow out of. How many times have we had someone pray for us or we have prayed for someone else and we saw or even felt things change? There is power the world barely understands, but to the Christian it makes perfect sense and that power is made available by sharing experiences.

Look at the story of the Tower of Babel in Genesis 11:1-6.

Genesis 11:1–6 (NKJV) ***Now the whole earth had one language and one speech*****. And it came to pass, as *they* journeyed from the east, that *they* found a plain in the land of Shinar, and *they* dwelt there. Then *they* said to one another, "Come, let us make bricks and bake them thoroughly." *They* had brick for stone, and *they* had asphalt for mortar. And *they* said, "Come, let us build ourselves a city, and a tower whose top is in the heavens; let us make a name for ourselves, lest we be scattered abroad over the face of the whole earth." But the Lord came down to see the city and the tower, which the sons of men had built. And the Lord said, "*Indeed the people are one* and they all have one language, and this is what they begin to do; *now nothing that they propose to do will be withheld from them.*"**

God Himself made a profound statement here. He said in verse 6, "*Nothing they propose to do will be withheld from them.*" Think about that—*nothing*! The fact that they were doing this together gave them power to do something they could never do by themselves. We read another story in the Old Testament where people sharing an experience caused the presence of God to manifest in an incredible way.

2 Chronicles 5:11–14 (NKJV) And it came to pass when the priests came out of the Most Holy Place (for *all the priests* who were present had sanctified themselves, without keeping to their divisions), *and the Levites* who were the singers, all those of Asaph and Heman and Jeduthun, *with their sons and their brethren*, stood at the east end of the altar, clothed in white linen, having cymbals, stringed

instruments and harps, and *with them one hundred and twenty priests* sounding with trumpets—indeed it came to pass, when *the trumpeters and singers* were as one, to make one sound to be heard in praising and thanking the LORD, and when *they* lifted up their voice with the trumpets and cymbals and instruments of music, and praised the Lord, saying: "For He is good, for His mercy endures forever," that the house, the house of the Lord, was filled with a cloud, so that the priests could not continue ministering because of the cloud; for the glory of the Lord filled the house of God.

Notice the house of the Lord was filled with a cloud because everyone shared the experience of worshiping God. The experience of worshipping *together* caused the presence of God to manifest in a stronger measure. I believe in being in the presence of God in my own prayer time and experiencing God alone. But no matter how good God's presence is alone, there is something greater when I worship alongside someone else. Call it the corporate anointing, unity or whatever you want to call it, but it is a spiritual principal. There is power when people worship God together. It brings about a power we can't achieve alone. In fact, this became a pattern in the book of Acts.

Acts 1:14–16 (NKJV) *These all continued with one accord* in prayer and supplication, with the women and Mary the mother of Jesus, and with His brothers. And in those days Peter stood up amid the disciples (*altogether the number of names was about a hundred and twenty*), and said, "Men and brethren, this Scripture had to be fulfilled, which the Holy Spirit spoke before by the mouth of David concerning Judas, who became a guide to those who arrested Jesus; for he was numbered with us and obtained a part in this ministry."

Acts 2: 1–3 (NKJV) When the Day of Pentecost had fully come, *they were all with one accord in one place.* And suddenly there came a sound from Heaven, as of a rushing mighty wind, and it filled the whole house where they were sitting. Then there appeared to them divided tongues, as of fire, and one sat upon each of them.

Acts 4:23–31 (NKJV) And being let go, *they went to their own companions* and reported all that the chief priests and elders had said to them. So when *they* heard that, *they* raised their voice to God *with one accord* and said: "Lord, You are God, who made Heaven and earth and the sea, and all that is in them, who by the mouth of Your servant David have said: 'Why did the nations rage, And the people plot vain things? The kings of the earth took their stand, And the rulers were gathered together against the Lord and against His Christ.' For truly against Your holy Servant Jesus, whom You anointed, both Herod and Pontius Pilate, with the Gentiles and the people of Israel, were gathered together to do whatever Your hand and Your purpose determined before to be done. Now, Lord, look on their threats, and grant to Your servants that with all boldness they may speak Your word, by stretching out Your hand to heal, and that signs and wonders may be done through the name of Your holy Servant Jesus." And *when they had prayed*, the place where they were assembled together was shaken; and *they were all filled with the Holy Spirit, and they spoke the word of God with boldness.*

Two times here in the early stages of the Church we read about the shared experience of prayer causing the Holy Spirit to manifest in an incredible way. It brought power to the ministry of the apostles and the rest of the 120 that they had not attained on their own. Now we are not talking about young, still ignorant Christians, but the disciples and some of the multitude that had followed closely the teachings and ministry of Jesus.

They had taken His "yoke" upon them. A yoke, in those times, besides being a device for holding oxen together for plowing, was a term used to describe the mentoring process that an older priest would give to a younger follower. The person took the yoke of the mentor and learned everything he knew. These disciples had learned everything Jesus had taught them for three years. Now they were ready to go and unleash that on the world, but it took them obeying Jesus words of staying put, *with the others,* until they were given the power to give that yoke to the world.

What if one of them had decided not to stay with the group? He knew as much as the next person who was there with Jesus. He had seen the same miracles, the same multitudes, the same crucifixion, and the same resurrection. Even so, it was still the power of the *shared experience* of waiting for the Holy Spirit to be given, that gave them the power to go and do what they were called to do. I believe that if one of them had gone off on his own, he wouldn't have received that power and wouldn't have shared in the incredible birthing of the Church until he had shared the experience of "receiving power" as Jesus called it.

In the second account, they were threatened to stop teaching using Jesus' name. So, they took the time to regroup, share another prayer experience, and worship God. It was at this point the shared experience caused them to be filled again with the Holy Spirit and go out and preach with more boldness.

These shared experiences gave much power to the early church!

Even Jesus taught us about the power of the shared experience.

Matthew 18:19–20 (NKJV) "Again I say to you that if *two of you* agree on earth concerning anything that they ask, it will be done for them by My Father in Heaven. For where *two or three* are gathered together in My name, I am there in the midst of them."

I believe the presence of God is inside each Christian and we are not alone because He is with us. However, I believe His power is stronger and can manifest more when believers have shared experiences together in being part of the Church. I believe it has to do with how God made us and goes back to His original intent.

Besides a piece of God being inside of us, we're all a small part of our ancestors and parents. We are made from other human beings which causes us to all be somewhat tied together biologically. Because we are tied together biologically, all our bodies can pick up the "energy," "current," "power," or whatever you want to call it, from others.

It has been proven that the brain and heart both give off electrical current. In the earlier study, they have now seen it and can measure it. I believe our bodies, even though natural, are "wired" to receive or transmit power from, or to, those around us. Therefore, we are affected by the atmosphere we put ourselves in. This is especially true when the atmosphere has other people in it. Shared experiences with other people should be carefully selected because the power shared will affect you.

When you go to a public event, do you ever see the person leading the event encouraging everyone to have a terrible time, hate the person next to you, and be disgusted by everything? No. Usually public events are positive because, even though we haven't always understood it, we are wired to pick up what others are giving off.

While at an event, the behavior of a few people can ruin it for others. I remember being at a Cincinnati Reds game at the old Riverfront Stadium. Ken Griffey, Jr. was playing for the Reds then and they were playing the St. Louis Cardinals, with Mark McGuire. The Reds were losing thanks to a massive homerun from McGuire. As the game got into the later innings, someone three sections away from us had become so intoxicated and unruly that they started a fight. This fight spilled out into the aisle and more and more people were yelling, getting involved, and watching what was going on.

This attention spread section by section until we couldn't help but see and be moved by what was happening. The action of those people was turning the whole area of the stadium toxic. We were all so involved in the upheaval that we totally forgot what was going on in the game. This positive shared experience was being tarnished by the actions of someone else.

We were not only irritated by the scene and the energy being given off, we totally missed the game getting tied with a homerun by Griffey. A person with a couple of thousand people between us sent such negative energy out that grew and grew and grew to the point people could see and feel it.

When election time comes around, almost everyone strongly dislikes negative campaigning because it personally affects us. Have you ever been in a good mood and after a few minutes of being around a negative person you feel the same way? Or vice versa? Other people will affect us because our body is a conduit for power to flow through.

When people, as a group, are having a positive experience, it creates an atmosphere of positivity. Therefore, the Church is the ultimate shared experience. When we get together to worship our God, we shouldn't be bickering about church politics, even though I believe in protecting the interest of the church. We shouldn't be lowering the hammer on volunteers or staff who didn't quite get a cue about the lights or audio in the service, although I believe in excellence. We shouldn't be worrying about who's trying to spread gossip or split the church, although I believe in protecting the sheep and correcting errors.

We should be creating a positive spiritual experience that spreads the power of God to those who come to within a proximity of our church. We want the positivity to be so strong it swallows up the negative to the point it can't continue.

Sadly, we don't see that.

We have seen threatened, stressed out, and borderline burned-out church leaders who are negative about what is going on in their world. They aren't creating a positive shared experience for the people who come in the door. These people need a positive change, and what ends up happening is the power that is transferred back and forth is negative. The cycle continues and we see people leaving the church never having experienced the full change God intended for them to have.

God created our bodies not just for natural fellowship, but also for exchanging power. One of the keys to being everything God has created us to be is creating positive shared experiences with other believers and allowing that power of "like faith" to strengthen, encourage, change, mold, teach, heal, and affect us in a way we need in our lives. This power should be cultivated amongst believers in the Church and then exposed to the unsaved in the world. This is how people come to want what the Church has.

However, for us to show it, we must be filled with it. And to be filled with it, it requires regular involvement in the local church. Let's share the Spirit of God that changed our lives with each other and watch other's lives change as well!

You Are a Vital Organ

To achieve the full Christian life, we must *become* a part of a local church and not just be satisfied knowing we make up the global Church. Paul said that being a part of the local church was like being a vital organ in a body. Most organs are so vital that the body cannot live without them. The local church is a body and you are key to it living and growing and thriving. You are a vital organ like the heart, the brain, the liver, the lungs, etc.

If an organ is to survive, it must be inside of and connected to a body with proper blood flow. Those organs can only survive outside the body, in stasis for a brief amount of time. The same is true for you as a believer. You were made to fill a specific role just like the lungs are meant to pass oxygen, or the heart is meant for the flow of blood, or the brain to tell all these things to do their job. The person who does not commit to being part of a local church is missing out on some of the spiritual filling.

Romans 12:4-5 (NLT) Just as our bodies have many parts and each part has a *special function*, so it is with Christ's body. *We are many parts of one body*, and we all belong to each other.

Eventually, an organ that is removed from the body, even in stasis, will die. An organ cannot live outside of the body and neither can you. Those who refuse to become part of a local body are robbing themselves of a full ¼ of their spiritual tank being full. This is also the first visible sign that someone is on the decline and are most likely not filling themselves with the first half of the tank at home anyway. That's right, when someone becomes inconsistent at church and being around other believers, it is a symptom (not always) that the other parts of the tank are not filling either. Of course, I'm not talking about those who cannot be there because of work or other occasional and understandable reasons. I am referring to those who simply do not go because they do not see the importance of it, are convinced they do not need it, *always* have something more important to do, have talked themselves into believing they can get all they need on their own, or simply just do not like being around people.

Ephesians 4:16 He makes the whole body fit together perfectly. As each part does its own special work, it helps the other parts grow, so that the whole body is healthy and growing and full of love.

Being a part of the local church, and for that case, the family of God, is not something that can be looked at as unimportant. The Church is full of individual people following God's plan for their lives that come together to make up a corporate plan that God has for the world. This is imperative for you to fill this ¼.

The Solution

The church is the solution for us to have the relationships God wants us to have and us to fulfill our role as a vital organ in the body of

Christ.

Acts 4:32–35 (NKJV) Now the multitude of those who believed were of one heart and one soul; neither did anyone say that any of the things he possessed was his own, but they had all things in common. And with great power the apostles gave witness to the resurrection of the Lord Jesus. And great grace was upon them all. Nor was there anyone among them who lacked; for all who were possessors of lands or houses sold them, and brought the proceeds of the things that were sold, and laid them at the apostles' feet; and they distributed to each as anyone had need.

Therefore, the church is so important—to be part of filling believers—because the world needs every one of the members of the body and their story. I have heard other people say, "The Christian experience is dead."

I am here to say with a loud voice that *the world needs full Christians and the Church to fulfill God's original intention*. The world isn't giving natural shared experiences anymore. People are not reaching out and touching each other in a way that is natural and nourishing.

The church is the place that encourages social interaction, spiritual interaction, and need-meeting interaction; not a place where people come just to fulfill their spiritual duty and make them feel better about themselves. It wasn't created to be a place where people come to get "topped off" as they go back into the world.

Today, people have crazy schedules and less and less time, but that's the whole point of why they stay empty. The Church is the ultimate shared experience where believer's come to understand they need God, but also for them to share God with each other! By doing this, all believers are becoming well-rounded in their walk with Him. By taking some of the time that so many have less and less of, they are investing into their lives, relationships, spiritual health, and future. They are filling themselves the way God intended.

Don't be secluded away from the world to pray and seek God! Get involved with other members of the body of Christ! In the words of Jesus, "Go into *all the world and preach the gospel to every creature."* (Mark 16:15, NKJV)

The Church is a place where you can experience the greatness of another person demonstrating the greatness of God. When I say the greatness of another person, I am not talking about the greatness of their success, but the greatness of what a relationship with people who know Jesus Christ as their Lord and Savior can be—a place where my relationship with another believer shows me a side of God I haven't experienced yet.

Church is a place where we can all come together and share experiences on every level of life. We can share experiences in our relationships with God, and share experiences that help us become the incredible people God created us to be. It's the place where needs are met physically, emotionally, and spiritually. There isn't a better place for the ultimate shared experience.

CHAPTER 12

Church is Where You Hear the Word Preached and Experience the Power of God as a Family

Obviously, there are other places where we can hear good preaching and experience God's anointing, but those places aren't always the same place you experience with your church family. When you can build faith in a place where you have real relationships with people, that is where you can see the real benefit a local church has in your life. When you come to church, you and your church family hear the same word preached and the whole church's faith grows.

When I was a youth pastor in Tulsa, Oklahoma, I had a friend who worked in another department at the church. He would often come and see me during his afternoon break, and we would sit and talk in my office. He had served as a youth pastor along the eastern seaboard and was in the process of receiving his degree in leadership.

Listening to him talk would challenge me in ways I didn't enjoy because I didn't want to think about the things he'd talk about. I was busy with my own struggles of ministry at that level. It was a full-time job to keep my head straight with what I knew, but he would walk into my office, place a bomb in my brain, and then walk out. It was infuriating and awesome all at the same time. I had someone who had done what I had done, who was now working in the same organization as me, and he was still challenging me to change, grow, and understand more than what I had up to that point.

It was a direct result of those conversations that I decided to go back to school to get my business degree from Southwestern Christian University and ultimately my Doctorate from Faith Christian University. And this was all because someone had walked where I walked, lived where I lived, and challenged me to be more.

When I moved to Florida, a very good friend of mine who has an internationally-known ministry would invite me over to his house or we'd go grab a bite to eat or go see a movie. When we are together, he constantly causes me to get out of my comfort zone. Just being around him and listening to him pushes me to improve.

This book is a direct result of listening to him talk about being booked all over the world at some of the largest and best churches, being gone 30 to 40 weekends a year, and still having enough time to write two books and start a third. He lives where I live, doing something like what I do (just on a grander scale), and has a wife and family. He encourages and strengthens my faith because He relies on God to constantly take him to the next level.

These two examples are the power of the local church when it comes to building your faith and experiencing the power of the Holy Spirit.

Romans 10:14–15 (NKJV) How then shall they call on Him in whom they have not believed? And how shall they believe in Him of whom they have not heard? And how shall they hear without a preacher? And how shall they preach unless they are sent?

It is imperative to hear someone else preach the Word. If you are not hearing someone else expound on the Bible, I guarantee you have a lopsided, "you version" (not the Bible smart-phone app) of the Word and who God is. A local church, where you can put down roots and become a part, is a place that preaches the Word for the world and community in which you live. Sometimes the pastor may be preaching a message that a person in that community absolutely needs to hear at that very moment in their life.

When a minister lives in the same community, sees the same challenges, and walks with you through the fire, he is seeking God about the same things which you are wondering. Spirit-led and Word-based messages will always produce fruit and faith in your life. What does it take on your part? It merely requires listening and application.

A local church may preach something you don't like, or may rub you the wrong way. However, many times those abrasive messages are the very ones you need to hear to fill you in ways you haven't been filled before. But it's not just abrasive messages that fill you up. It's also when they are encouraging, elementary, boring, or sermons that make you feel good about yourself.

Feel-good messages or messages in an area where you feel confident or close to God are not causing growth and maturity as much as you think. Sure, we all want to hear messages we can agree with, but how can we grow if those messages are never challenging? *We will never learn or grow past what challenges we are willing to face.*

And the local church can help with that because it preaches to the very world in which local people are living! If you want to see how God looks at your community, attend and join a local church that preaches God's Word. Your faith for your community will grow if you will listen and connect.

The local church is also the place where power is released for that community, on a regular basis.

Hebrews 10:24–25 (NLT) Let us think of ways to motivate one another to acts of love and good works. And let us not neglect our meeting together, as some people do, but encourage one another, especially now that the day of his return is drawing near.

Matthew 18:19–20 (NLT) I also tell you this: If two of you agree here on earth concerning anything you ask, my Father in Heaven will do it for you. For where two or three gather together as my followers, I am there among them.

Acts 2:1–4 (NLT) When the Day of Pentecost had fully come, *they were all with one accord in one place.* And suddenly there came a sound from Heaven, as of a rushing mighty wind, and it filled the whole house where they were sitting. Then there appeared to them divided tongues, as of fire, and one sat upon each of them. And they were all filled with the Holy Spirit and began to speak with other

tongues, as the Spirit gave them utterance.

There is tremendous power available when believers get together. In the church world, we like to throw around big theological sounding words, and one that applies here, we're going to discuss. When believers get together and worship God, they experience the "corporate anointing." (There's no doubt this term came straight from the "Christianese" dictionary.)

The corporate anointing is the term describing the power and presence of God each of us have on the inside that's coupled with the power and presence of God in others when we get together.

Let's analyze the term just a little more. Everyone who is a Christian has some measure of the power and presence of the Holy Spirit. The Bible calls this measure, "the anointing."

2 Corinthians 1:21–22 (NKJV) Now He who establishes us with you in Christ and has *anointed us* is God. Who also has sealed us and given us the Spirit in our hearts as a guarantee.

1 John 2:20, 27 (NKJV) But *you have an anointing* from the Holy One...But the *anointing which you have received from Him abides in you...*

Every believer has the anointing. It is that anointing that can be coupled with the anointing in other believers to increase the anointing (the power and presence of God) in the church. When this unity happened throughout the Bible, the presence of God showed up in unusually powerful ways.

2 Chronicles 5:11–14 (NKJV) And it came to pass when the priests

came out of the Most Holy Place (for all the priests who were present had sanctified themselves, without keeping to their divisions), and the Levites who were the singers, all those of Asaph and Heman and Jeduthun, with their sons and their brethren, stood at the east end of the altar, clothed in white linen, having cymbals, stringed instruments and harps, and with them one hundred and twenty priests sounding with trumpets—indeed it came to pass, when the trumpeters and singers were as one, to make one sound to be heard in praising and thanking the Lord, and when they lifted up their voice with the trumpets and cymbals and instruments of music, and praised the Lord, saying: "For He is good, For His mercy endures forever," that the house, the house of the Lord, was filled with a cloud, so that the priests could not continue ministering because of the cloud; for the glory of the Lord filled the house of God.

In the Old Testament, the temple of God was a man-made building or tent, and the glory of God was a cloud in which God covered Himself. This was a common occurrence in the Old Testament. These verses were a very unusual manifestation of God's presence and power. It was so awesome that the priests couldn't stand up to do their job. In today's day and age, there have been some big changes made. However, the power and presence of God is still available to us to be filled in our walk with Him. Today the house of God is different. It's not a tabernacle. *It's the heart of every believer!*

Hebrews 3:6 (NLT) But Christ, as the Son, is in charge of God's entire house. *And we are God's house*, if we keep our courage and remain confident in our hope in Christ.

Believers are the house of God. I know many people look upon the structure of the actual church as God's house, but it isn't. Those structures are just buildings. We, as believers, are the house of God! In First Corinthians 3:16, the Apostle Paul wrote, *"Do you not know that you are the temple of God and that the Spirit of God dwells in you?"* (NLT). *The Amplified Bible* says, *"Do you not discern and understand that you (the whole church at Corinth) are God's temple (His sanctuary), and that God's Spirit has His permanent dwelling in you (to be at home in you, collectively as a church and individually)?"*

God wants to pour out His Spirit into every believer, and through every believer. He does not want to pour it out on a building because He wants to show Himself in the lives of us as believers. When we meet, the power and presence of God becomes stronger than if we have our own prayer meetings alone.

Chapter 13

Serving the Church!

Hebrews 6:10 (KJV) For God is not unrighteous to forget your work and labor of love, which ye have shewed toward his name, in that ye have ministered to the saints, and do minister.

Jesus Himself, lived a life that was excellent! He operated in an excellence which caused thousands to follow Him around. He had an upper level staff of 12 and a lower level staff of 120 that pulled off some incredible things, seeing as there was no television, computers, planning meetings, accounting software, or anything else. That excellence was most evident, not in the size of His meetings or even in the miracles He performed, but in the fact that everything Jesus did was done from His desire to serve mankind.

Jesus served mankind until the point of His death. Everything He did wasn't for His benefit, but for the benefit of every human being! This is important to believers who want to be filled.

If Jesus served, it's an example to all that we should be serving as well. This is how the world will see God's love through the body of Christ. It isn't in the beauty of the building, the eloquence of the messages, or the manifestation of the anointing as much as it will be the service we give to others.

To some people, the words "servant," "service," or "serving" are demeaning and derogatory. Many view it as an entry-level thing and instead want "important" roles if they are going to get involved in the church. Serving is not something anyone is too good to do. When done correctly, all the "important" ministry roles—preaching, singing, or being on the stage in front of people—are done from a heart to serve people.

Jesus is and always will be our example. Look at what He said about Himself in Matthew 20:28, *"For even the Son of Man came not to be served but to serve others and to give his life as a ransom for many."*

Jesus healed because He was serving sick people. Jesus preached because He was serving people with no hope. Jesus washed the disciples' feet because He was serving His disciples.

Serving in church causes believers to sow into the lives of people God has called us to share life, experiences, and space with at church. God is the one who rewards our serving. The person serving doesn't reward themselves and neither do the people they are serving.

In Everything You Do, You Must Be Serving Someone in Your Life

As believers, we are called to serve every person we encounter. Even our employees, employers, kids, family members, and spouses are targets to receive our serving. It is important to understand that serving has nothing to do with reward or pay. To "minister" to someone is the Greek word "diakoneo," which means preaching and teaching, but it also means serving to meet the needs of people to show the goodness of God.

What is a need? Many people will automatically think financial. This is how we usually try to meet needs. If we hear that someone has a need, we usually reach for our wallet to give them something. But needs aren't purely financial.

There are plenty of needs that can be met with no money changing hands at all. People need love, acceptance, patience, friends, opportunities, helping hands, advice, encouragement, a listening ear, a reference for a job, and so much more. Serving allows us an opportunity to meet those needs. If the church is the ultimate place to share experiences that show us more of God in each other, then serving other believers is a chance to make that happen in a way people can tangibly experience. And even though it feels like you are giving out, you are making room to be filled even more!

The Church Needs More Than Preachers

1 Corinthians 15:58 (NLT) So, my dear brothers and sisters, be strong and immovable. ***Always work enthusiastically for the Lord, for you know that nothing you do for the Lord is ever useless.***

It's obvious when someone goes to church, they will experience the pastor, associate pastor, music pastor, or maybe even the children's and youth pastor. These titles are obvious and it seems they carry some importance because they oversee certain areas of the church. However, the largest part of ministry that takes place in the body of Christ happens through those serving! This is known as the ministry of helps and this is where every believer, who isn't called to preach from the pulpit, is called to serve.

Serving is the largest and most vital role in any church. There is nothing greater than serving. Without believers serving, the other ministerial gifts can't function. If you want to be filled and live a full Christian life the way God intended, you can find no better place to make that happen than serving!

Jesus needed help in His ministry. If that is true, how can serving be belittled or looked down upon? Serving in the church is the largest ministry of all because the more effective the serving, the more influence, resources, and reach the church will have.

Believe it or not, all believers are a product of someone else's serving. The preacher may have been the one who talked them the rest of the way in, but it was the serving of hundreds of others that kept the door to the church open, the sanctuary clean, the buckets to receive the offering passed, the lobby set up, the sound system turned on, the instruments played, and the words on the screen. It was prayer groups who prayed for those who came and prayed for the service. It was volunteers meeting to make their church better, as much or more than anything the minister had to say.

Therefore, it is important for a believer to serve in a church. This is a direct way to minister to others who need ministry. When a believer serves the needs of others, they are making room for more of God in their lives. When they take their minds off their problems and start helping others, God always meets their needs. Need proof? Let's look in

First Kings.

1 Kings 17:8–16 (NLT) Then the Lord said to Elijah, “Go and live in the village of Zarephath, near the city of Sidon. I have instructed a widow there to feed you.” So he went to Zarephath. As he arrived at the gates of the village, he saw a widow gathering sticks, and he asked her, “Would you please bring me a little water in a cup?” 11 As she was going to get it, he called to her, “Bring me a bite of bread, too.” 12 But she said, “I swear by the Lord your God that I don’t have a single piece of bread in the house. And I have only a handful of flour left in the jar and a little cooking oil in the bottom of the jug. I was just gathering a few sticks to cook this last meal, and then my son and I will die.” 13 But Elijah said to her, “Don’t be afraid! Go ahead and do just what you’ve said, but make a little bread for me first. Then use what’s left to prepare a meal for yourself and your son. 14 For this is what the Lord, the God of Israel, says: There will always be flour and olive oil left in your containers until the time when the Lord sends rain and the crops grow again!” 15 So she did as Elijah said, and she and Elijah and her family continued to eat for many days. 16 There was always enough flour and olive oil left in the containers, just as the Lord had promised through Elijah.

Because the widow woman in this story obeyed God’s command to sustain Elijah, God met her need. When she humbled herself, and served the prophet of God, God took care of her *over and above her need.* Jesus said something very similar when He said, *“Seek the Kingdom of God above all else, and live righteously, and He will give you everything you need.”* (Matthew 6:33, NLT)

If you are trying to fulfill the need of living a full Christian life the way God intended, part of that involves serving in a local church! Anointing and higher callings are always associated with small beginnings.

Serving Always Leads to You Becoming Greater

Numbers 12:3 (NLT) Now Moses was very humble—more humble than any other person on earth.

John 3:30 (NLT) He must increase, but I must decrease.

Moses started off humble, backwards, shy, and stuttering. But he became one of the greatest examples of leadership and law givers in the history of the world. His image is the only biblical example to hang on the walls of the Supreme Court.

His humility can also be described as meekness. Meekness is part of nine things that Jesus said all Christians should have and show. The Bible calls them fruits of the Spirit. We can call them signs of being filled.

Meekness is what allows the door of promotion and blessing to be open *for* a believer instead of them forcing it open themselves. A believer who serves, *will always increase* when they look for a way to help.

Luke 14:11 (NKJV) For whoever exalts himself will be humbled, and he who humbles himself will be exalted.

1 John 3:16–17 (NKJV) By this we know love, because He laid down His life for us. And we also ought to lay down our lives for our brethren. But whoever has this world's goods, and sees his brother

in need, and shuts up his heart from him, how does the love of God abide in him?

Much like communion, serving is an outward expression of what is in a believer's heart. It is love demonstrated. When someone loves, they are making room for more of God's love in their life.

Matthew 23:11–12 (NLT) The greatest among you must be a servant. But those who exalt themselves will be humbled, and those who humble themselves will be exalted.

This verse says, if you want to be great in the kingdom of God, you must serve. Believers must lay down their lives, their plans and desires, and serve the church and its people.

What Does It Mean to Serve?

Sadly, there have been many lopsided teachings concerning this subject that have made people gun-shy. There have been church leaders who have taken advantage of the goodness many people have in their hearts and have abused and overworked their people. I do not subscribe to that school of thought.

I believe that if you see a need in your church that you can fill, you need to fill it! Why? Because when those needs are met, you immediately affect people! Every need is important, every person is valuable, and every chance to serve is an opportunity for you to be filled even more! But it's also important to serve at the pace you can.

I used to weigh 378 pounds. I lost 100 plus pounds thanks to several things. I was blessed to have lap band weight loss surgery, but I also started eating healthier, and working out. One thing I did, which was such a foreign concept to me, was start running.

I played football, basketball, threw shot put in track, and was a very active teenager, but if I didn't have to run, I didn't. Even during practices, I would hear my coaches yelling, "Bailey! Get in shape and hustle!" I was never a runner, but nonetheless, I started jogging.

I met a guy who was the definition of a runner. He ran marathons and nearly qualified for the Boston Marathon. I was trying to figure out a pace for myself that I would benefit from, but not be so uncomfortable that I would want to quit. This man told me, "If you can run and maintain conversation speech, that's the perfect pace."

That was exactly what I needed to hear. Today, I know I am going too fast if I can't articulately speak. I may look like a wild man running down the streets of my neighborhood talking out loud, but that's how I know I can go faster or if I need to slow down.

In the same way, this is what you need to do to pace yourself when it comes to serving. Many will start and want to do more than they can do. The eagerness to almost make up for lost time will cause many to overcommit. Don't do that. You should look at your schedule and the need that is present and work something out. When you serve as you can, you are meeting a need *and* filling yourself the way God intended.

Full Mark – Showing the Love of God

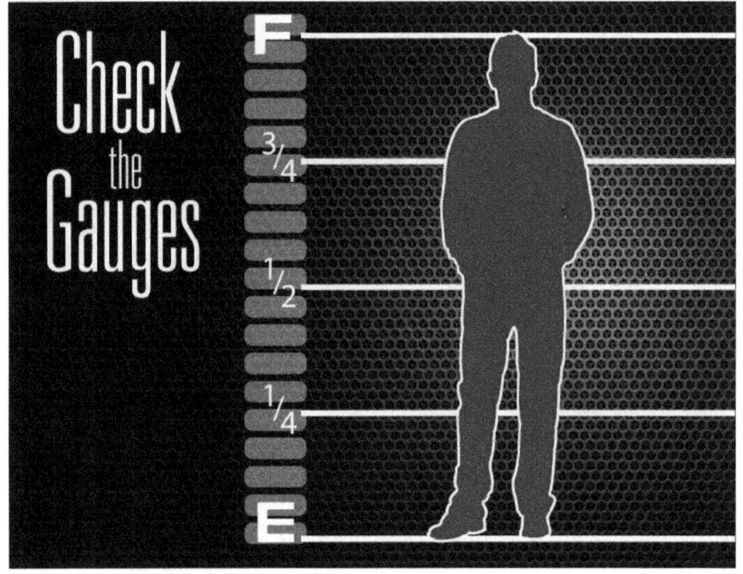

Chapter 14

The Greatest

As we approach the full mark, this is where we really separate the men from the boys and the women from the girls. This section is no doubt the hardest level to accomplish, but by far the most rewarding. This level is where you begin to separate your desires and natural reactions and discipline yourself to stop doing whatever you feel like doing. This step is showing others the love of God.

1 Corinthians 13:13 (NLT) Three things will last forever—faith, hope, and love—and *the greatest of these is love*.

1 John 4:8 (NLT) *He who does not love does not know God*, for God is love.

Neither Paul, who wrote First Corinthians, or John, who wrote First John, pulled any punches here. They both make some very powerful statements that put showing the love of God into perspective. First, Paul says love is the greatest gift of all. John follows it up by saying that if someone doesn't show the love of God, they don't know God at all. Then he tells us the reason—because God is love. If you do all the rest of the things we have talked about in the first ¾ of your spiritual tank, but do not show others the love of God, *you become "nothing,"* no matter how successful you may become in any area of your life. This step is saved to the last because without it, all the rest will not get you as far without it. Imagine going on a trip with only ¾ of the tank filled. You don't make it as far as with a full tank, do you?

Before I go on, let's look at what love is. Since I pastor just a few miles down Interstate-4 from Disney World, there is a very popular idea of love that is portrayed all the time—the romantic, fairy tale, prince charming version of love. It's everywhere! All the Disney princesses parade around the Magic Kingdom singing, "Some day, my prince will come."

This version of love comes from the Greek word "eros," which is a romantic and physical love. This is where the world gets the word "erotic." Obviously, one expression of romantic love is through the physical act of sex, but it is also shown in the form of affection, communication, emotional connection, physical touch, and the hearts of the people to become one. It is a romantic love.

There is another word that means love that every one of us experience. This love is love like a brother. This is the Greek word "philos," which is where the world gets the word "Philadelphia" from.

Philadelphia, of course, is known as the "City of Brotherly Love." This love is the kind of love enjoyed by family, friends, and others.

Both loves are rooted firmly in humanity. Both kinds of love have limitations on how much they will tolerate, how much they can be expressed, and both can be finicky based on how a person feels now.

But there is a third kind of love and that's what this section of the book is going to explore. This type of love is the Greek word "agape," which means the unmerited love God shows to every human being. He showed all of creation and especially humanity this love by sacrificing His only Son, Jesus, to make the world right with Himself. He performed such an incredible gesture with no guarantee anyone would accept it. That is how much God loves us!

That sacrifice was enough to satisfy God's judgement and allow humanity to continue to live, have a pathway to redemption, and have hope when challenges come their way. Human love is not capable of doing that. Eros and philos are selfish because they focus on what they want and what makes the one showing the love, feel good. Agape love focuses solely on what it can do for the person receiving the love.

Love Is the Greatest of All

I have stated several times that I was born and raised in Kentucky. We are blessed in "The Bluegrass State" to have many famous people from there. Amongst a list a mile long dominated by country singers, Kentucky also has famous politicians such as President Abraham Lincoln, explorers and settlers like Daniel Boone, and actors such as Captain Jack Sparrow himself, Johnny Depp, and George Clooney. However, many people do not know that one of the greatest and influential sports figures was also born there. Cassius Marcellus Clay, Jr. a.k.a. Muhammed Ali was born in Louisville. What is the point of telling you that? Ali had a poem in 1963 called "I Am the Greatest."

> "I Am the Greatest...By Cassius Clay. This is the legend of Cassius Clay, the most beautiful fighter in the world today. He talks a great deal and brags indeed-y of a muscular punch that's incredibly speedy. The fistic world was dull and weary. With a champ like Liston, things had to be dreary. Then someone with color - someone with dash - brought fight fans running with cash. This brash, young boxer is something to see. And the heavyweight championship is his destiny. This kid fights great. He's got speed and endurance. But if you sign to fight him, increase your insurance. This kid got a left. This kid got a right. If he hits you once, you're asleep for the night. And as you lie on the floor while the ref counts 10, you pray that you won't have to fight me again. For I am the man this poem is about, the next champ of the world, there isn't a doubt. If Cassius says a cow can lay an egg, don't ask how. Grease that skillet. He is the greatest. When I say two, there's never a third. Betting against me is completely absurd. When Cassius says, a mouse can outrun a horse, don't ask how. Put your money where your mouse is. I am the greatest."

In every interview and public appearance, Ali was not shy about his opinion of himself. Most of it was hype, but this opinion is shared now by many fight analysts and greatest boxers of all time. I saw an interview with Mike Tyson where he agreed that Ali was the greatest. Whether he is or isn't will always be a source of opinion, skepticism, and endless hours of debate amongst boxing fans. "Just because he said he was the greatest doesn't mean he really was, does it?" The guess work will always be there. The Bible mentions many gifts that are available to us. Ministry gifts, spiritual gifts, ability gifts and so on. These gifts are given to cause and show spiritual growth in our lives. When it comes to what is the greatest evidence of true spiritual growth in your life, love is it!

Paul starts off the most famous wedding scripture in the history of the world with some pretty big bombshells. He says everything believers are called to do what amounts to nothing, if they don't treat others the way God treats them.

1 Corinthians 13:1–3 (NKJV) Though I speak with the tongues of men and of angels, but have not love, I have become sounding brass or a clanging cymbal. And though I have the gift of prophecy, and understand all mysteries and all knowledge, and though I have all faith, so that I could remove mountains, but have not love, I am nothing. And though I bestow all my goods to feed the poor, and though I give my body to be burned, but have not love, it profits me nothing.

Boom! Spiritual bombshell! Just a chapter before and even a chapter after, Paul talked about the gifts of the Spirit. He instructed the church in Corinth how these things should operate. Paul was telling believers they should have access to these things, both as recipients and as those who administer them.

To allow the gifts of the Spirit to make their full impact, God placed them inside a filter that would ensure their effectiveness. Look again at what Paul says if the gifts of the Spirit aren't ministered through the filter of the love of God. They become useless.

1 Corinthians 13:1–2 (NKJV) Though I speak with the tongues of men and of angels, but have not love, I have become sounding brass or a clanging cymbal. And though I have the gift of prophecy, and understand all mysteries and all knowledge, and though I have all faith, so that I could remove mountains, but have not love, I am

nothing.

Paul is saying that the "gifts of the Spirit" should be *filtered* through the "fruit of the Spirit," of which love is named first, or they are wasted gifts. If the gifts of the Spirit need to be filtered through love, then who are we to think that every other action shouldn't be filtered through that same love?

Even if you are correct in your argument, belief, or theology, if you don't show the love of God, will anyone receive it? Nothing else has a greater impact on people than that. No spiritual manifestation, relevant sermon, outstanding worship, cool lobby and coffee bar, no instantaneous miracle, or dramatic outpouring will impact anyone's life greater than the love of God. This passage of scripture tells us that these other things will disappear, dissipate, and cease, but the love of God will never end.

What is the Love of God?

If the love of God is the greatest force on the planet, we should know what it is. Immediately thoughts come to mind; how to treat people, acts of kindness, taking care of the poor, and so on and so on.

Before I say anything else, please understand I am not saying that these things are not love. Some Christians need to get a handle on these basics of showing God's love. I am appalled sometimes at how many Christians do not know how to treat people. I see believers who don't tip (at least not very well) their servers at restaurants, they fight and argue at the drop of the hat, they are always wanting what they want regardless of how it affects other people. You know those shopping cart corrals in store parking lots? To use one of those is a far mystery for them. They just let the carts roll. "Who cares" if it hits someone else's car? They will be rude, selfish, overly-opinionated, and sometimes just plain hateful towards people. Love, or the lack thereof, at its basic introductory level, is treating people the right way. Love *is* treating people kindly, performing acts of kindness, taking care of the poor, and so on. These acts should not be done simply because of what they do for us, but because we are showing the "fullness" of God to the rest of the world. This full mark shows more of what you have been putting inside!

The love of God is an attitude of the heart, not the act itself. For example, buying every member of the studio audience a brand-new car is awesome, unless the person doing it only did it because of how it made them feel. I'm not passing judgement on any of the talk shows that have done that. I am merely using that as an example.

When something is done with selfish motivation, in terms of spiritual development, it is wasted. The love of God is the *selfless* promotion of someone else. He is calling us, as believers, to love people that way and the more we do, the fuller our tank becomes.

Love is not based on how the recipient treats you when you are showing it. Christians have frequently missed it here. They are more focused on the reaction of the recipient, than the recipient themselves. The motivation of believers must first be rooted in a love that is not shaken by how the recipient responds.

In other words, the recipient's response is not the measuring stick of whether you are showing the love of God or not. People who need to be shown the love of God will respond with a variety of different reactions. If you base whether you're showing the love of God or not on their response, what happens if they respond wrong? Are you going to stop loving? Sadly, we all have done this at sometime in our life.

Here is the bigger question, "Can you still do something to better the life of someone else, no matter how negatively the recipient responds?" I am not talking about giving them everything and becoming a doormat for them to abuse and take advantage of you. I'm talking about loving them the way God does. Jesus died with no guarantee that anyone would accept what He did, yet He still died for everyone just to bless them. He paid the debt of sin for every person who would ever live. He didn't do this for Himself, but for all human kind.

People beat Him, spit on Him, laughed at Him, denied they knew Him, betrayed Him, doubted Him, and killed Him, yet He still did what He could do to make their lives better.

Nothing you can do for someone else will ever profit you spiritually, unless it is done from the motivation of God's love. Why does that have to be your motivation? It must be rooted in showing God's love because that is what He is. God *is* love!

1 John 4:8 (NLT) He who does not love (like God loves) **does not know God, for God *is* love.**

When you respond from a place of being concerned more for the other person than yourself, you are quite literally applying the love of God to yourselves *and* to the recipient. *Both are literally being touched and affected by God Himself.*

The greatest way to apply God to any situation is by selflessly promoting the lives of others. When someone crosses your path, they should leave in a better state.

When I was growing up, my grandfather, Howard Bailey, had a small shed full of tools that could perform a variety of different tasks. When I say full, I mean filled to the rafters. He had everything from shovels, hammers, surveying equipment, hoses for siphoning gasoline and a funnel to put it back in, a million screws, nuts, bolts, nails, wrenches, screwdrivers, and everything in between.

If one of his grandchildren had to borrow something, he was adamant about it being put back where we got it. In fact, his words were crystal clear, “Put it back where you found it, in better shape than when you got it.” That meant, even if it was already dirty from the last person who used it, when we were finished with it, it shouldn’t be dirtier. It was cleaned, including the dirt that may have already been on it when we borrowed it. None of us used those tools because we wanted to clean the tools or organize his shed. *We used them because we needed the benefit of the tool*. However, when all of us learned to leave them in better shape than how we found them, it didn’t take too long to notice we found them in better shape, lasting longer, and able to serve a greater purpose than a broken, tangled, dull, rusty tool.

This is what showing the love of God does for all of us as believers. We aren’t searching for the difficult people to show God’s love to because we want to be around difficult people. We show the love of God to someone because they desperately need the same love that was shown to us.

To enjoy that benefit, we need to leave everyone we come across in better shape than before we found them. When that happens, both the giver and receiver are experiencing God directly. If we would do this, it will not take long to start seeing the improvement of this world and the people in it!

If someone did something to you that deserves the benefit of the doubt, give it to them. If someone did terrible things to you, forgive them. If someone is annoying and hateful, love and pray for them. Always do what is necessary to apply God directly to the situation because both parties will be directly touched by Him. It is by doing this, believers make room for God to take care of and fill them.

Proverbs 25:21–22 (NLT) If your enemy is hungry, give him bread to eat; And if he is thirsty, give him water to drink; For so you will heap coals of fire on his head, And the Lord will reward you.

I say this with all confidence, God will take care of and reward that kind of behavior!

Why Believers are Not Seeing More Rewards

Like anything in your relationship with God, it is a process. Many times, people are afraid to show God's love too much because they don't want to be taken advantage of and end up with nothing.

That shows me two things. First, people don't understand what showing the love of God is. They will put the understanding of past experiences and a filter of their life on what showing love is. Showing the love of God is not just a series of actions, in and of themselves, it is loving like God does. More on that in a bit.

1 Corinthians 13:3 (NKJV) And though I bestow all my goods to feed the poor, and though I give my body to be burned, but have not love, it profits me nothing.

People are trying to do things out of a sense of human understanding instead of allowing the Holy Spirit to lead their actions. The love of God is best shown through His leading. It is always, however, for the betterment of others. Although every believer, as I said earlier, should be showing kindness to people, the larger and specific acts of love should be administered by the Holy Spirit's leading. Showing God's love is a whole lot more than you might think it is. It is something that should be done by the Holy Spirit's leading so that *your* motivation stays selfless.

For example, if I know someone has a large financial need and I have the means to meet it, does that mean I'm automatically supposed to meet it? Unless the Holy Spirit is leading me to, the answer is no. What if God didn't want me to do it? What if He was trying to stretch someone else's faith to step out and sow a seed into that person's life? If so, I've stolen that opportunity from them. Not to mention, that person might start to doubt that they heard from God.

On the other hand, people will use the excuse of "not being led" to keep from doing things they should be doing all the time. If you can find direction in the Word (which is why I said the Word should be put into the tank first), then that is all the leading you need.

For example, Proverbs 18:24 says, "*A man who has friends must himself be friendly.*" (NKJV) So I do not need to "be led" to be friendly to people. The Word tells me I should be anyway. I know that to have friends, I must be friendly. However, the Holy Spirit can lead me on how close of a friendship I should have with certain people. Some relationships I have should keep certain limitations; others I can allow closer; and others I'll allow into my "inner circle." But those people are only getting closer and ultimately into the "inner circle" by the leading of the Holy Spirit.

The second reason believers aren't seeing more rewards of showing God's love is they don't believe it will do any good, change the situation, or set themselves up for blessing and growth. This simple fact remains—applying love to a person is applying God directly to the heart of both the giver and receiver. The last time I checked, God is always successful and will never fail. So, what does that mean? The Christian who is administering the love of God must believe and expect the reward of showing that love in their life.

No Love = No Faith

The Apostle Paul shows every one of us something so relevant and eye-opening that it has the potential to shake us to our core.

Galatians 5:6 (NKJV) For in Christ Jesus neither circumcision nor uncircumcision avails anything, but faith working through love.

Paul is telling us that the outside doesn't mean too much. What causes our faith to *work,* is how much we show the love of God to others.

Several chapters ago we mentioned that our faith is what causes everything in God's kingdom to be received and enjoyed. Some have said that God gives everything freely, by grace. That is true. A relationship with God is given freely by grace. However, *what God gives freely by grace must be grabbed by faith.* Our faith is the only thing that can accept the things of God in our lives.

Here is the part you *must* understand: *Faith doesn't work without the selfless promotion of someone else.* Faith is *purely dependent* on love! We can't treat other people judgmentally, poorly, or unfairly and expect our faith to still work.

There are some blessings of God that people are not enjoying because they need to improve how they show the love of God to others. Even if the promise is in His Word, they won't see that promise become a reality in their life if they aren't showing the love of God to people because their faith will not be *able* to grab it! Their "hands" are tied.

Some people need to forgive someone they are completely justified in being upset with. Others may need to tip their servers better at restaurants, even when they received bad service. Some need to stop talking about people like dogs behind their back simply because that person is not as spiritual as they think they should be.

I could keep naming things, but the bottom line is this: If you are not loving people the way God loves, with no guarantee of reciprocation, you are causing your faith not to work. If your faith isn't working, you are not growing closer to God, not enjoying the blessing of God, and that lack of faith is affecting your reward from God. The more selfless promotion of someone else you can show, you will see your faith continue to get stronger and your tank will fill up!

Showing God's Love is How Others Will Know We Believe

John 13:35 (NLT) Your love for one another will prove to the world

that you are my disciples.

As the full mark starts to come into view, it is important to emphasize that the way you will know you are reaching it is not by your ability to perform miracles, see visions, or have and give a powerful testimony. It is not by overcoming a checkered past or being healed of tremendous emotional or physical sickness. It will not be from your impressive vocabulary of Christian words, crying in the presence of God, or the fish decal you put on your car. You will know simply by the love you have for another!

To truly promote someone else selflessly cannot be done without God's love. Some believers get confused by this because they are still applying human love standards to this equation.

If you have two number threes and the answer you need is nine, then addition is not what you need. Multiplication is required to turn two number threes into the number nine.

Human love isn't what is needed to selflessly promote someone else. The Church can't show the world that they are His disciples by simply doing kind acts of human love. While it isn't wrong to desire people to come to our churches, only helping people who agree to come to our church is based on human love. Helping anyone, whether they come to your church or not, is based on God's love.

How can you know the difference? Human love seeks its own benefit. Believers showing merely human love will tell someone else they love them, because of how it makes them feel. *Gifts given out of human love are always beneficial to the giver.*

God's love will treat people kindly without expecting to be treated kindly in return. God's love will do things for people without a condition. God's love will tell someone they are loved without needing to be told the same in return. This love will not selflessly promote the recipient because they deserve it, but because this kind of love will make the recipient's life better.

1 John 3:14 (NKJV) We know that we have passed from death to life, because we love the brethren. He who does not love his brother abides in death.

If you have a hard time showing this, you are still looking to your own interpretation of love. God's love does not dwell in intellect where everything makes sense. God's love does not dwell in flesh and emotions where the feelings are. God's love only dwells in the heart and can be accessed by faith.

You must look deeper into your heart and use your faith to show it to someone else. *This is the only evidence of salvation.* You can tell someone you are a Christian and that your tank is full, but the only evidence of being a Christian and having a *full* tank is by showing God's love to others. If you are born again, the love of God is in your heart. You must believe and expect this love to manifest for it to work in your life.

Love's Arch Enemy

If you turn on the television, talk to pretty much anyone, or don't live with your head in the sand, you can tell that there is a lot of pain and suffering in the world. While we know that Jesus is the only hope for all of humanity, there is a simple cause for why Jesus had to come. This simple cause that brings about all pain and suffering, just so happens to be the arch enemy of love.

2 Timothy 3:1–6 (NKJV) But know this, that in the last days perilous times will come: *For men will be lovers of themselves*, lovers of money, boasters, proud, blasphemers, disobedient to parents, unthankful, unholy, unloving, unforgiving, slanderers, without self-control, brutal, despisers of good, traitors, headstrong, haughty, lovers of pleasure rather than lovers of God, having a form of godliness but denying its power. And from such people turn away! For of this sort are those who creep into households and make captives of gullible women loaded down with sins, led away by various lusts.

Love's arch enemy is mentioned right there is verse two: *For men will be lovers of themselves*. This means to love yourself more than anyone else or to put it simply, become selfish. Love's arch enemy is selfishness. Selfishness is not a fish you can eat. Being selfish is the cause for everything bad the world is facing today.

Adam and Eve committed the original sin because what they wanted became more important to them than what God wanted. Here is something every human being needs to understand: We are all born selfish. It comes in many different forms that is gets by unrecognized: children taking each other's toys, a desire to look better than somebody else, the secret jealousy when someone else gets blessed, and so much more.

There is nothing wrong with wanting to do something as well as you can. There is nothing wrong with wanting to be the best version of yourself. However, it becomes selfishness when you are pleased that someone else fails so you can get to the place you want to be.

All forms of selfishness are bad. When someone thinks of not being selfish any more, it usually triggers the thought, "*What if I am taken advantage of?*" Even though there is nothing wrong with being cautious, that thinking is still selfish.

Your faith needs to stay in God's Word and what it promises. If God says He will reward someone who loves like Him, He will! God will take care of, restore, and cause His Word to always work for those who believe Him.

Being Selfish is Something That is Chosen

I'm going to say something right here that may cut against the grain of what we are referring to; but to love someone else you do have to properly love yourself first.

Mark 12:29–31 (NLT) Jesus replied, "The most important commandment is this: 'Listen, O Israel! The Lord our God is the one and only Lord. And you must love the Lord your God with all your heart, all your soul, all your mind, and all your strength.' The second is equally important: '*Love your neighbor as yourself.*' No other commandment is greater than these."

I believe you can't love someone else if you don't have a healthy and proper love for yourself. I know you might think of all your shortcomings, faults, and things you believe are so horrible about yourself that no one could or would love them.

This book is not about self-image, but I will say this: a person who believes in Christ is not the person they were before. The Bible calls them a new creation and all the things in their life that were seemingly unlovable have been replaced (spiritually speaking, on the inside) with the character of God. The more they continue to reach the full mark in their life, the change on the inside will start to show on the outside!

Even though we as believers are called to love ourselves so we can love someone else, the larger truth is *no one is called to love themselves so much that they only care about themselves*. To show the love of God, you must realize that you must selflessly promote someone else instead of selfishly promoting yourself.

I could tell you story after story of buying things for people for Christmas or birthdays only to have that person take my present back. Part of me has been offended no matter how often it happens. I asked myself why that was and this is what I have determined: When I buy something for someone else, I'm buying them something *I* want them to have. I am not necessarily buying what they want.

Advertisers trick the public with this all the time. The masses are tricked into believing they want a variety of items because they are told they want it. I believe it was Jerry Seinfeld who said he was never so surprised to hear these words come out of his mouth at three o'clock in the morning, "Yes, I'd like to order the Ginsu knife."

The advertiser's trick is to get a person to believe they want what they are selling. The truth is the person wants what they are selling because that is what they are being told. In the end, the advertiser is giving the person what they want them to have, not necessarily what the person wants or even needs. Make no mistake about this fact, if it is for sale, a company is not trying to sell someone something they need. The company is selling what they want the consumer to have.

To truly show the love of God, you can't bless the recipient with what you want them to have. You must consider what the wants and needs of the recipient are and ignore what you want. The recipient may receive it with gladness, gratefulness of heart, and gratitude. Or they may be offended, ungrateful, take it back, or reject it all together. If you are administering the love of God, you can't be shaken either way. Your job was merely to offer betterment to that person's life, selflessly. Once this is accomplished, this quarter of your tank is filled and you start to live your life the way God intended.

Chapter 15

Identifying the Look and Benefit of Love

In 2004, my father in law, Bob, gave Jodi and me a hot tub. It was an older acrylic hot tub, but it was huge, didn't have any leaks, and just needed a new pump, heater, and hose connections. I had never done any work on a pool in my life, let alone plumbing or electrical. I was, however, raised on a construction job in the summers, working for my dad. I probably knew enough to be dangerous.

I didn't have the money it would take to install and rewire this massive, six-person tub, so I started with what I knew I could do. I built walls that would hold it up. Next, I ordered the pump, heater, and hoses. When they arrived at my house, I became confused. None of it made sense to me. I didn't even know where to begin. I was tempted to give up and just start saving money until I had enough to hire someone to fix it.

Thank God I found an installation manual in the box. I started with page one, step one and began cutting hose, priming, gluing hoses to jets, and making connections. I eventually got all but three jets hooked up, and to make a long story short, I got the plumbing finished and hooked up the heater and pump.

I moved onto the wiring of the electrical system. Because I believe you must respect electricity, I got everything connected to the point of putting it onto the breaker box. It was at that point I called my cousin Aaron, who had spent summers working with his dad doing electrical work. We got it all hooked up and, lo and behold, it worked.

Even though my friends made fun of me and told me I was wasting my time, I stayed with the directions. The instructions were incredibly valuable to me and I could achieve my goal.

This is very much like showing the love of God. To do so, you should know how to know how. Thank God there is an instruction manual. He has given us what it looks like to selflessly promote someone else in First Corinthians.

Love Puts Up With "Stuff" For a Long Time and is Kind

1 Corinthians 13:4–7 (NKJV) Love suffers long and is kind; love does not envy; love does not parade itself, is not puffed up; does not behave rudely, does not seek its own, is not provoked, thinks no evil; does not rejoice in iniquity, but rejoices in the truth; bears all things, believes all things, hopes all things, endures all things.

It's not very appealing to start off with the words "suffering long," but that is where the whole thing begins. *Strongs* tells us the word suffer means "to endure patiently under someone's action or speech that is annoying or makes one angry, especially when it is deliberately from someone else." Could that be any less appealing?

When it comes to dealing with other people in life, a lot of us are quick to give them a moment of time, but if they don't measure up, we are quick to move on. If the situation calls for the two of them to be around each other, there is usually a sense of *I'm only doing this because I have to. I have to love you because I'm a Christian. I'm only doing this to help you. Don't get used to this.*

I'd say pretty much everyone "suffers long" around other people in some way because everyone is so diverse in who they are. Spouses will suffer long for each other and are usually very quick to point that out. Some people at work may have others treat them poorly or they get passed over for a promotion. Usually these people are very quick to trash their coworkers or complain about them to their friends.

The fact is, people do treat each other poorly. But to show the love of God, you must put up with this and be patient and kind while doing it. A good question to ask yourself is, "How patient and kind is God with all of humanity?" When you are ready to cut someone off in traffic, sever a relationship, or give someone a piece of your mind, think of how many times God wanted to do that same thing with you, but doesn't. You must take a deep breath and ask for God's help. Whether your patience runs out over a simple difference or a major falling out, the love of God can still be shown and you *can* be patient and kind. This is just the first step to topping off your tank.

Love Is Not Jealous or Proud

1 Corinthians 13:4b (NKJV) Love does not envy; love does not parade itself, is not puffed up.

Envy and pride are two sides of the same coin. Envy is a feeling of being resentful, a longing aroused by someone else's possessions, qualities, or luck. When you are constantly looking at what someone else has been blessed with and wishing it was yours, you are not showing the love of God.

There is a way to identify envy so you will know if you have fallen into it. First, you will often be offended by someone else's blessing causing jealousy to arise. Many will ask and say, "Why did they get that?" "I've been here longer." "Those people aren't even saved." "I've worked harder." "They aren't even honest." "Why are they being blessed?" This is simply devaluing the recipient of the blessing, to put you in a place where you can tolerate the fact someone other than you got blessed.

The other way to identify envy is recognizing when you begin to expect the person who received the blessing should bless you too. You might begin to think the person is the answer to your prayer. You might even quote the Word to yourself and say, "God is going to supply my need through them because of the big blessing they just received."

When I was a youth pastor, I saw this frequently. It was not uncommon for us to raise money to help kids who wouldn't have had the money otherwise to go to our camps, retreats, and events. There was a family one year who came and told us they didn't have the money and there was no way their son could go to camp. We placed him on the sponsorship list and helped him go so he could experience the life-changing power of God in an event like summer camp.

The day of camp arrived and we loaded the bus for the ranch where we hosted our camp. This young man stepped on the bus with a brand-new pair of Air-Jordan sneakers and a brand-new wardrobe for camp. When asked about not having any money, his response was, "Well not for something like this." When people begin to look at other people as the answer to their prayers, that's a pretty good signal they are being envious. At that point, they are not showing the love of God.

The other side of the coin is pride and arrogance. I believe there is nothing wrong with celebrating when blessings come! These are the times you shout hallelujah, raise your hands, and thank God for it. However, shoving your blessing in the face of someone else is not showing the love of God.

If someone tells you how nice one of your possessions is and your response is, "Yeah, you should've seen the price tag," that is a response based in pride. When you believe for one second you deserved the blessing or you are good enough to receive the blessing, that is a response based in pride.

Pride can be defined as believing a lie about oneself. No person has ever deserved or been good enough to receive or expect God's blessings on their own. The only reason any good comes into anyone's life is because of what Jesus did. Period. If God didn't have a plan to get humanity back, there would never be blessings. Ever!

If you are jealous of someone or are bragging all the time, that is not showing the love of God, and your tank is never going to be full.

The Love of God is Not Rude or Selfish

1 Corinthians 13:5 (NKJV) Does not behave rudely, does not seek its own.

Showing the love of God is not rude to other people, even if they have been rude to you. It is amazing how many people will use that as a defense for their own rude behavior. *Strongs* defines rude as, "to behave unbecomingly; to be in an unfinished state or rough, like a term paper that isn't finished yet; lacking refinement or delicacy; offensive in manner or actions; marked by or suggestive of lack of training or skill; ignorance of or indifference to good form; it may suggest intentional discourtesy." To be sure, showing the love of God does *not* mean you have arrived at a state of perfection, a state of being finished, or a state of refinement; it does not mean you are fully trained, or have a perfected skill.

Showing the love of God is *acting like you have, even though your thoughts and emotions want to say otherwise*. There is a time coming when believers will be completed, perfected, trained, taught, and have good form. That is what filling the tank is striving for. Showing the love of God covers all that up in the meantime.

Ephesians 4:11–16 (NLT) Now these are the gifts Christ gave to the church: the apostles, the prophets, the evangelists, and the pastors and teachers. Their responsibility is to equip God's people to do his work and build up the Church, the body of Christ. This will continue until we all come to such unity in our faith and knowledge of God's Son that we will be *mature* in the Lord, measuring up to the *full and complete* standard of Christ. Then we will no longer be immature

like children. We won't be tossed and blown about by every wind of new teaching. We will not be influenced when people try to trick us with lies so clever they sound like the truth. Instead, we will speak the truth in love, growing in every way more and more like Christ, who is the head of his body, the Church. He makes the whole body fit together perfectly. As each part does its own special work, it helps the other parts grow, so that the whole body is healthy and growing and full of love.

When you are rude, you are letting out what you (and most likely everyone else) is thinking. Showing the love of God doesn't mean you didn't think it, didn't want to think it, or never thought it. Showing the love of God is choosing to not act like it and show how unfinished and untrained you might be.

How in the world can you do that? Because love is not looking for what it wants.

Love is not only not rude, but it is also not selfish. A person showing the love of God does not put their desires first. You do this by helping someone else get what they want instead of working against them. Let people get in line first. Put the shopping cart in the corral in the parking lot instead of letting it roll wherever it may roll. Let someone else talk first and don't try to top their stories.

Placing others' needs ahead of your own is how love is released. A great measuring stick to see if this is happening can be found by the way someone starts a sentence. If many of your sentences begin with, "I want… I did… I think… etc.," that's a good sign you are seeking your own interests.

Let me add this so we don't take this train of thought into a ditch: Jesus did say it is okay to want some things. I don't want you to think it is not okay to believe for some of your desires.

Mark 11:24 (NLT) I tell you, *you can pray for anything*, and if you believe that you've received it, it will be yours.

However, if you are only taking care of all your needs with your faith or are making sure everyone else knows what those needs are, where are you leaving room for love? When someone is doing something and you think you can do it better, you are not leaving room for love if you move them out of the way to show how well you can do it.

Showing God's love is not concerned with what only it can do, only what it wants, or what its rights are. It is the selfless promotion of someone else. The less you lean on your desires, the more your tank starts to fill with the goodness of God.

Love Does Not Keep Score

The *Amplified Bible* says it this way, "(Love) is not touchy or fretful or resentful; it takes no account of the evil done to it." I'm sure many people read that and say, "Whatever! How can I forget that? They don't deserve my forgiveness!"

I know when something is hurtful, there is a part of that experience that is somewhat beneficial. When you remember how something felt, you can protect yourself from it happening again, but to become overly sensitive is to remove the love of God from being shown, thus stunting your growth. *Strongs defines* the word touchy as, "irritated or incensed to anger; to allow someone else to drive one to anger."

Showing the love of God makes room for others to fail so you can "love them out of it." You must ask yourself how touchy, fretful, and resentful you are. How much are you noticing what people are doing wrong to you? This is the gauge by which you can tell if you are showing the love of God or not. If you are keeping score of everything done wrong to you, then you are not showing the love of God and therefore keeping yourself from reaching the full mark.

What do I mean by keeping score? Are you fully aware of what is being done to you to the point you have magically discerned the heart and intentions of the other person? Isn't that called judging? Isn't it funny that we judge others by their actions but judge ourselves by our intentions? Showing the love of God means you believe when someone else does something, it may not have been as bad as you think.

Love Gets Happy Over the Truth

1 Corinthians 13:6 (NKJV) Does not rejoice in iniquity, but rejoices in the truth.

There are some Christians who are excited about the fact that hell is a real possibility for arrogant people who believe differently than we do. That should never be a point of celebration no matter how badly those people may treat any believers.

If you are to achieve a full life the way God intended, that fact cannot be a point of celebration. When people in the world have bad things come their way, why would any Christian be happy about that?

I've heard with my own ears Christians say, "That's what they get" with a smirk on their face. Remember, the selfless promotion of someone else should be trying to make everyone's life better! No matter how much bad a person has done, a Christian should never be okay with the knowledge that anyone is deceived and could end up in hell.

Some might say, "But they've done so many horrible, mean, and nasty things. Don't they deserve that?" Who are we to decide that? Did you deserve it? Did you want the bad you sowed in your life to be harvested? We as believers should always be praying for others to experience the truth of Jesus' death and resurrection so we can celebrate with them the fact the truth is now in them.

The more "good" someone experiences in their life, the more apt they are to do good to others. Believers should be praying, hoping, and believing for good to come into the lives of others so they can become whole and impact the world positively. That is why showing God's love celebrates only in the truth.

Love Believes the Best of Everyone

1 Corinthians 13:7 (NKJV) Bears all things, believes all things, hopes all things, endures all things.

As we close in on the last quarter of a tank, which is brutal to our flesh, I believe this one is the most important. It's believing the best about everyone. The *Amplified Bible* reads this verse like this:

1 Corinthians 13:7 (AMP) Love bears up under anything and everything that comes, is ever ready to believe the best of every person, its hopes are fadeless under all circumstances, and it endures everything [without weakening].

The words "bears up under anything" mean that showing the love of

God will endure without divulging to the world that it's hard. It literally means to not let water inside of something and floating on top of it, like a boat.

If you are going to show the love of God, you must believe the best about everyone. What does that mean? To believe the best even when things may have come out the worst. Showing the love of God believes for good, even when it is not so obvious. Believe in the good until it is proven, beyond a shadow of a doubt, it is not.

Love does not jump on the bandwagon of assumption. Give people the benefit of the doubt instead of jumping to negative conclusions. There are people who keep tabs and form an arsenal against people, just in case. They're kind of like a computer back up, because they are convinced that something bad is going to happen, and so they are constantly gaining ammunition. These people will involve themselves in gossip just to add fuel to the fire. The sad part of that is, these same folks want everyone to give them the benefit of the doubt they aren't ready to give to anyone else.

God is always ready to believe the best about all of us because of Jesus restoring us to that place. God still believes that humans can do better. If you are always believing the worst about people you encounter, go to church with, family members, you are not sharing the love of God and will never reach the full mark.

Refuse to believe bad reports about others until it is proven otherwise. The response of "I knew they were like that" or "I'm not surprised," is stopping the love of God from flowing out of your heart and you are slowing down your own growth, understanding, and filling!

That kind of action is contributing to someone else's downfall and sowing seed for that to come back in your life.

The Benefits

1 Timothy 4:8 (NLT) Physical training is good, but training for godliness is much better, promising benefits in this life and in the life to come.

The Bible encourages believers to make love your goal. Not only should you be striving for it, but becoming it! If this is something God desires for every believer, there must be a reason. Anytime God does something; it is never just for your benefit. Even though showing the love of God benefits the receiver, as I said earlier, it benefits the giver as well. Showing God's love is His way for us to achieve a full life in spirit, soul, and body.

Showing God's Love Is Profitable

Showing God's love is the godliest thing a believer can do. Paul told Timothy that showing God's love is an idea that illustrates His will. Exercising does profit some. As I told you earlier, I lost a lot of weight through a combination of lap band surgery and literally working my butt off in the gym. When Paul said bodily exercise is good, but training to be godly is much better, what did He mean?

Exercise will only pay off in this life. Working to be like God in all things will be profitable now and in Heaven. The word profitable means beneficial, useful, and *yielding a return that creates circumstances that increase the chance of success.*

When you show the love of God, you are bringing about a return on the investment you are making into the other person, which increases the chance of your success. When is the increase of that success for? It is for your life right now on the earth! It will also increase your reward in Heaven! Showing the love of God pays off now and then!

1 Timothy 4:8 (NLT) "Physical training is good, but training for godliness is much better, promising benefits in this life and in the life to come."

Love Allows the Power of God to Flow Freely in and Through You

Mark 11:25–26 (NKJV) "And whenever you stand praying, if you have anything against anyone, forgive him, that your Father in Heaven may also forgive you your trespasses. But if you do not forgive, neither will your Father in Heaven forgive your trespasses."

Jesus drops a huge bomb right here. He states that if a believer is showing the love of God, their prayers will be answered.

I stated earlier that showing the love of God is a sure-fire way to get your faith to work. I know a lot of people who are believing God at His Word and still haven't seen their prayers answered. The question someone at this stage should ask themselves is are they showing the love of God and forgiving someone who has wronged them? Jesus emphatically says that if they don't, the Father will not forgive them.

If there is something between you and God, His hands are tied and He cannot answer your prayers. That's kind of a big deal, isn't it? If your prayers can't be answered, then you should be looking at showing the love of God towards people the way God showed His love toward you.

1 Peter 3:8–11 (NKJV) Finally, all of you be of one mind, having compassion for one another; love as brothers, be tenderhearted, be courteous; not returning evil for evil or reviling for reviling, but on the contrary blessing, knowing that you were called to this, that you may inherit a blessing. For "He who would love life and see good days, let him refrain his tongue from evil, And his lips from speaking deceit. Let him turn away from evil and do good; Let him seek peace and pursue it."

1 Peter 3:8–11 (AMP) Finally, all [of you] should be of one and the same mind (united in spirit), sympathizing [with one another], loving [each other] as brethren [of one household], compassionate and courteous (tenderhearted and humble). Never return evil for evil or insult for insult (scolding, tongue-lashing, berating), but on the contrary blessing [praying for their welfare, happiness, and protection, and truly pitying and loving them]. For know that to this you have been called, that you may yourselves inherit a blessing [from God—that you may obtain a blessing as heirs, bringing welfare and happiness and protection] For let him who wants to enjoy life and see good days [good—whether apparent or not] keep his tongue free from evil and his lips from guile (treachery, deceit). Let him turn away from wickedness and shun it, and let him do right. Let him search for peace (harmony; undisturbedness from fears, agitating passions, and moral conflicts) and seek it eagerly. [Do not merely desire peaceful relations with God, with your fellowmen, and with yourself, but pursue, go after them!]

Peter says that the power of God can flow through a believer and they may receive a blessing! You can't be showing the love of God and trash talking someone. You cannot have unforgiveness in your heart and show the love of God at the same time. If that is the case, God's power cannot flow in and through you because you are doing evil.

1 Peter 3:12 (NKJV) For the eyes of the LORD are on the righteous, And His ears are open to their prayers; But the face of the LORD is against those who do evil.

But when the power of God is flowing freely, without anything to slow it down, you not only selflessly promoted someone else, but you will see your prayers answered, your health maintained, your youth renewed, your marriage in bliss, your friendships will be solid, you will understand the Bible better, and your life increasing in all other areas.

Conclusion

Fill Up Regularly

Well, here we are at the end. This is the place I pray you've reached. Like I said at the opening of this book, in 1987 when I first started driving, I had a 1987 Firebird. This car had a 14-gallon tank. Over the years, I have had many different cars with different sized tanks. Currently, at the time of this writing, I am driving a 2009 Cadillac Escalade ESV that has a 32-gallon tank. Obviously, it takes more gasoline to fill up the Cadillac than it did to fill up the Firebird. It may take a little longer and cost a little more to fill it up, but the benefit is I can drive a lot further and cover many more miles.

This is how it's going to be in your walk with God. Right now, you may not understand much of the Word, you may not know everything to say when you pray, or your attention span may not allow you to spend hours with God. Maybe your priorities aren't to be at church every time the doors are open. Perhaps you may not have a lot of love of God to share with people.

Where you are at on the journey right now is irrelevant. The point is, fill yourself as much as you can right now. Fill your tank to the limit! Allow God's grace to empower you to grow and obtain your fullness right now. Here is the best part: You will grow and your tank will get bigger and eventually the actions you are taking to fill your tank now, that you find challenging, will become easier and will not be enough to fill your spiritual tank in the future. Just keep filling with these things more and more. One day on your journey, you'll look back and be amazed at just how far you've come!

I pray for you and believe that your life will become filled the way God intended for those who follow Him to be filled. Your life will take on a whole new dimension and I am so excited for you to become the version of yourself that God intended you to be. “Fill ‘er up” and get on the journey!

In closing, I want to speak a blessing over you that I speak over my church every week. I call you blessed! I say you’ll go everywhere God has called you to go! You will have everything God has created you to have! You will do everything God has called you to do! And you will be everything God has created you to be! You will walk in the favor of the Lord and your life will be blessed! Let’s go take the #journeytogether!

ABOUT THE AUTHOR

Brent Bailey is founder and lead pastor of Direction Church in Orlando, Florida. There is nothing better for Brent than his wife and sons, the Kentucky Wildcats, peanut butter milkshakes, and ministering to people. Since accepting the call to ministry in 1991, Brent has a real passion for people establishing their own relationship with God because "It's easy to receive from someone you know." Pastor Brent has a Doctorate in Ministerial Leadership from Faith Christian University in Orlando, Florida, a Bachelor in Business from Southwestern Christian University in Bethany, Oklahoma, an Associate Degree in Theology from Faith Theological Seminary in Tampa, Florida, and received a diploma in Pastoral Ministry from RHEMA Bible Training College in Tulsa, Oklahoma. Brent and his wife Jodi have been married since 1999, and have two incredible sons, Preston & Peyton.

www.ingramcontent.com/pod-product-compliance
Lightning Source LLC
Chambersburg PA
CBHW061819040426
42447CB00012B/2725

* 9 7 8 0 6 9 2 8 5 0 5 8 9 *